AQA Accounting

AS

Exclusively endorsed by AQA

David Austen
Peter Hailstone

 Nelson Thornes

Published in 2008 by:
Nelson Thornes Ltd
Delta Place
27 Bath Road
CHELTENHAM
GL53 7TH
United Kingdom

08 09 10 11 12 / 10 9 8 7 6 5 4 3 2 1

A catalogue record for this book is available from the British Library

ISBN 978 0 7487 9869 8

Cover photograph by Alamy

Page make-up by Fakenham Photosetting, Norfolk

Printed and bound in Slovenia by Korotan

Acknowledgements
Photo p.v Getty Images

Contents

Introduction

Nelson Thornes and AQA

Nelson Thornes has worked in collaboration with AQA to ensure that this book offers you the best support for your A level course and helps you to prepare for your exams. The partnership means that you can be confident that the range of learning, teaching and assessment practice materials has been checked by the senior examining team at AQA before formal approval, and is closely matched to the requirements of your specification.

Blended learning

Printed and electronic resources are blended: this means that links between chapters and activities between the book and the electronic resources help you to work in the way that best suits you, and enable extra support to be provided online. For example, you can test yourself online and feedback from the test will direct you back to the relevant parts of the book.

Electronic resources are available in a simple-to-use online platform called Nelson Thornes learning space. If your school or college has a licence to use the service, you will be given a password through which you can access the materials through any internet connection.

Icons in this book indicate where there is material online related to that topic. The following icons are used:

Learning activity

These resources include a variety of interactive and non-interactive activities to support your learning, such as Drag and drop activities and Worksheets.

Progress tracking

These resources include a variety of tests that you can use to check and expand your knowledge on particular topics (Revision quizzes) and a range of resources that enable you to analyse and understand examination questions (On your marks…).

Worked example

These resources provide step by step help on how to work through a particular accounting skill.

When you see an icon, go to Nelson Thornes learning space at www.nelsonthornes.com/aqagce, enter your access details and select your course. The materials are arranged in the same order as the chapters in the book, so you can easily find the resources you need.

How to use this book

This book covers the specification for your course and is arranged in a sequence approved by AQA.

The book content is divided into chapters and topics that match the AQA Accounting specification for Units 1 and 2 – Financial Accounting and Financial and Management Accounting. Chapters 1–4 cover Unit 1 and Chapters 5–11 cover Unit 2.

The features in this book include:

Learning objectives

At the beginning of each chapter and topic you will find a list of learning objectives that contain targets linked to the requirements of the specification.

Key terms

Terms that you will need to be able to define and understand.

Case study

An overarching business scenario, to be used throughout a topic or chapter.

Illustration

A worked example that will show you how to go through a particular accounting skill.

■ Activity

Suggestions for practical investigations you can carry out, these will help you to test your knowledge and understanding

■ Background knowledge

An extension to the main text that will provide you with added bits of useful knowledge.

■ Links

This highlights any areas where topics relate to another part of this book, or to the A2 specification.

AQA Examiner's tip

Hints from AQA examiners to help you with your study and to prepare for your exam.

AQA Examination-style questions

Questions in the style that you can expect in your exam appear at the end of each topic and chapter.

AQA examination questions are reproduced by permission of the Assessment and Qualifications Alliance.

Learning outcomes

A bulleted list at the end of each topic or chapter summarising the content in an easy-to-follow way.

■ Web links in the book

Because Nelson Thornes is not responsible for third party content online, there may be some changes to this material that are beyond our control. In order for us to ensure that the links referred to in the book are as up-to-date and stable as possible, the web sites provided are usually homepages with supporting instructions on how to reach the relevant pages if necessary.

Please let us know at **webadmin@nelsonthornes.com** if you find a link that doesn't work and we will do our best to correct this at reprint, or to list an alternative site.

UNIT 1 Financial accounting

Introduction to Unit 1

Unit 1 is designed as the foundation of the course covering double entry procedures as applied to the accounting systems of sole traders, the verification of accounting records and the preparation of trading and profit and loss accounts and balance sheets. The lessons learned in this unit will form the solid foundations to be built on in your remaining studies.

The chapters in this section of the book follow the four sections of the syllabus:

As an introduction to the subject, **Chapter 1** looks at the reasons for keeping accounting records and the interests that stakeholders will have in these records.

Assessment could be based on the benefits to a business of maintaining accurate financial records or on identifying stakeholders and stating their particular interests in the accounting records.

Chapter 2 introduces the important rules of double entry bookkeeping that will be essential to all of your future studies in accounting and develops the necessary skills to enable students to identify source documents and account for these in the subsidiary books. Each subsidiary book is described in detail as is the process of posting from subsidiary books to the ledger system.

Candidates are expected to understand the different stages as a transaction passes through the accounting system, enabling them to accurately write up and close off day books, ledger accounts and cash books. In addition, candidates should be prepared for questions requiring them to identify the source document and subsidiary books that would be relevant to particular transactions.

Having processed transactions through the ledger system, **Chapter 3** details the important aspects of verification of the records by means of trial balance, bank reconciliation statements and sales and purchase ledger control accounts. In addition, the chapter addresses the issue of errors and error correction by means of the suspense account, together with assessing the effect that errors may have on profit calculations.

This section of the syllabus requires that candidates are able to understand the purpose and limitations of trial balances, control accounts and bank reconciliation statements as well as being able to prepare them. Candidates will be expected to identify different types of error, to assess what effect, if any, the error would have on profit calculations and to process corrections using a suspense account.

The final **Chapter 4** in Unit 1 builds on the knowledge acquired in earlier chapters and enables students to prepare the final accounts of a sole trader from a trial balance. The chapter introduces the concept of simple adjustments to both the final accounts and the ledger accounts in the form of expense prepayments, accruals and bad debts. Students will also learn how to adjust the final accounts for depreciation using the straight-line method.

Assessment may involve the preparation of all, or part of a set of final accounts involving closing adjustments. Candidates should be familiar with all presentational aspects of final accounts and be prepared to make the necessary amendments to an incorrect balance sheet.

Your examination will balance computational questions requiring, for example, the preparation of profit and loss accounts and balance sheets, control accounts or ledger accounts with written topics requiring you to identify or explain various accounting techniques or teminology.

In order to be successful in your examination, you must be very confident in your knowledge of the basic principles of double entry bookkeeping. This will enable you to confidently identify the debits and credits in a trial balance and correctly transfer these items into the final accounts. You may be presented with an incorrect trial balance or balance sheet and be required to prepare corrected versions of these. Once again, the key to this type of question is a sound knowledge of double entry principles.

Throughout the examination, candidates should be aware that they will be rewarded for good presentational skills and also that it is in their own interests to show workings wherever relevant.

Purposes of accounting

In this chapter you will learn:

- the reasons for keeping accounting records
- the benefits that arise for the owners of a business and other stakeholders.

Background knowledge

In practice, most businesses now keep their accounting records on computer, but computerised systems simply undertake all of the manual processes electronically. The processes we are studying for this unit are all manual.

Key terms

Profit: the amount by which income exceeds the costs of running a business in a trading period.

Trading account: calculates the gross profit made on sales by comparing the sales with the cost of sales.

Profit and loss account: calculates a business's net profit by deducting the expenses of running the business from the gross profit.

Balance sheet: a statement detailing all of the assets and liabilities of a business.

Stakeholders: individuals or organisations that have an interest (sometimes financial) in the organisation.

Link

For more information on cash budgets, see Chapter 10, page 157–9.

All businesses should keep accurate and up-to-date accounting records. These help the owners of the business to manage their affairs properly and enable outside stakeholders to assess how well the business is performing. This enables those stakeholders to safeguard their own interests. In this chapter you will learn the reasons why a business should keep these accounting records and also who these outside stakeholders are and what benefits they will gain from the accounts. Throughout your AS Level studies you should remember these reasons because they will help you understand the purpose of the various techniques you are going to study.

What are the reasons for keeping accounting records?

The practice of keeping accounting records goes back many thousands of years. In days gone by, traders would keep records of the money they spent and the money they received in order to see whether or not they had made a **profit**.

The same principles apply today, but clearly the scale and complexity of the accounting requirements has changed considerably as the scale and complexity of business has changed.

So, what are the reasons for keeping accounting records and the benefits to the owner of a business?

Recording and reporting what has happened in the past

All businesses need to be able to assess whether the business is profitable. Recording historic **income** and **expenditure**, and producing a **trading** and **profit and loss account**, enables this to be done.

Similarly, all businesses need to be able to assess whether they are solvent (i.e. do they have sufficient assets to pay all of their liabilities). Producing a **balance sheet** enables this to be done.

These reports enable **stakeholders** to be kept informed.

Forecasting for the future

Based on what has happened historically, owners are able to forecast what they anticipate will happen in the future, in the form of cash budgets or *projected* trading and profit and loss accounts and balance sheets.

Case study

Brian

Brian started his business as a baker three years ago and the business is expanding quickly. He has approached his bank for a loan to finance the expansion. And the bank has asked to see projected figures for the next year.

Link

For more information on projected trading and profit and loss accounts see A2 Module 4.

Key terms

Income: the value of resources recieved and recievable in the course of business.

Expenditure: the value of resources used by the business in acquiring goods and services.

Activity

Accounting information

Andrew has started a business selling car parts. List the information you would expect Andrew to keep records of.

Background knowledge

The accounts of a business will inform third parties of the performance of a business. These third parties, the stakeholders, need this information to make judgements about the business for various reasons.

Key terms

Liquidity: the ability of a business to access sufficient cash resources to pay its short-term liabilities.

Link

For more information on liquidity, see Chapter 9, page 147.

By looking at the trends of business for the past 12 months and assessing the business that he knows he has in the coming months, Brian will be able to prepare a projected profit and loss account to forecast the profit he will make, a projected balance sheet to forecast the condition of his business in the future and a cash budget to determine whether he will have a shortfall of cash in the coming months. This will enable Brian to identify the amount of finance he requires and the bank to ascertain whether Brian's business is a safe proposition as a borrower.

Monitoring and control

Accurate accounting records enable owners and managers to monitor what has actually happened in the business, compare this with what was forecast to happen and then take corrective action when necessary.

A legal requirement

Businesses have a legal requirement to maintain complete and accurate accounting records, principally to enable HM Revenue and Customs to collect all amounts due in respect of taxes.

Benefits to the stakeholders of a business

The individuals and organisations that have an interest in the accounts of a business are known as the stakeholders. They each have reasons for needing to know how safe and profitable the business is.

Owners

The owners of a business need to know whether the business is profitable and also to assess the **liquidity** of the business. Is the business generating sufficient cash to pay its liabilities in a timely fashion?

Managers

To enable managers to make decisions regarding the policies of the business, to plan for the future and to exercise control over the business. Without access to the financial statements, managers may inadvertently make decisions that are either not in the best interests of the company or are not practical in the light of resources that are available to them.

Suppliers

To assess whether the business is able to pay for the goods and services supplied according to the agreed terms.

Customers

To assess the continued viability of the business to meet their needs. In other words, will the business be able to supply goods ordered?

Providers of finance

Lenders, for example banks, finance companies, etc., need to assess whether the business can continue to meet its obligations to repay borrowings together with interest due on those borrowings.

Employees

To assess whether the business is able to continue trading and therefore continue to provide employment and pay wages that are due.

Government

To assess how much income tax and value added tax is due from the business.

Competitors

To assess how well their own business is performing in comparison. Does the competitor have higher sales, better profitability, etc.? This will enable competitors to identify problems in their own business and attempt to rectify them.

Potential investors

To assess the viability of investment in the business.

Local community

To assess the impact of the business on local community issues and the environment.

Case study

Recycle plc

Recycle plc is a multinational company with large plants throughout the world. The company has applied for planning permission to build a waste recycling plant on the outskirts of a village in Cornwall. The village is in an area of great natural beauty and relies very heavily on the tourist industry throughout the year. The local residents would be concerned as to the impact this would have on the local environment, on wildlife, on the business that tourists bring to the area and generally on the quality of their own lives.

Activity

Petroco

Petroco, a leading international petrochemical company has applied for planning permission for a processing plant on the outskirts of Hornbeach, a seaside town on the south coast of England. The company has organised a public meeting to gauge local opinion.

Detail the issues that are likely to be raised at the meeting.

AQA Examiner's tip

In question 1, be specific. Take each statement in turn and identify its purpose.

Learning outcomes

As a result of studying this chapter, you should now be able to:

- identify the reasons for keeping accounting records
- identify the main 'stakeholders' of a business
- identify the main reasons why the stakeholders of a business have an interest in the financial statements

---

 Examination-style questions

1 Andrew has been told that he should produce a trading account, a profit and loss account and a balance sheet at the end of his first year of trading. What is the purpose of **each** of these statements?

2 Andrew has been told that stakeholders will be interested in the final accounts of his business.
   (a)   What is meant by the 'stakeholders' in a business?
   (b)   List the stakeholders in a business and explain why they would be interested in Andrew's final accounts.

Accounting records: subsidiary books and ledger accounts

The basic principles of double entry bookkeeping are an essential skill that will be developed throughout your accounting course. The rules of double entry bookkeeping have been in existence for many centuries and most of the techniques and procedures you are going to learn rely very heavily on you having a good understanding of these rules.

This chapter will introduce you to the basic mechanics of double entry bookkeeping and introduce a number of terms that need to be remembered because they will occur throughout the course.

You will be introduced to the stages in the accounting process that are to be studied throughout this unit and will learn how to process a transaction from the beginning as a source document, through subsidiary books into the ledger system.

As you progress through your studies you will see that these basic principles remain unaltered and that all of the accounting techniques that you learn follow the same set of rules.

Source documents and double entry bookkeeping

In this topic you will learn:

- the basic mechanics of double entry bookkeeping
- how to recognise different source documents.

Double entry bookkeeping

All businesses must record transactions in their books of account. Double entry bookkeeping recognises that every transaction has a **dual aspect.** In other words, two accounts are affected and both sides of a transaction must be accounted for, th0e debit entry and the credit entry.

Each account has two sides – the **DEBIT** (on the left-hand side) and the **CREDIT** (on the right-hand side). These accounts are known as **T ACCOUNTS** and are set out in Figure 2.1.

The basic rule of double entry bookkeeping is that for every debit there must always be equal and corresponding credit(s).

When deciding which account to debit and which account to credit, you may find it helpful to recall the mnemonic '**DEAD CLIC**' (Fig. 2.2).

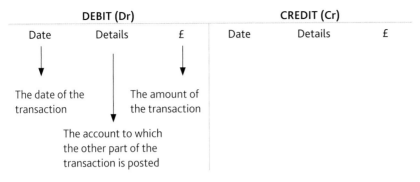

Figure 2.1 *T Accounts*

DEBIT (Dr)	CREDIT (Cr)
Expenditure	Liabilities
Assets	Income
Drawings	Capital

Figure 2.2 *DEAD CLIC*

The accounting equation

One of the most important fundamental principles in accounting is the accounting equation. This states that:

Assets – Liabilities = Capital

Assets are the resources that a business owns and uses to run the business and to produce and sell goods and services. Examples of assets are machinery, premises, stock and cash.

Liabilities are amounts that the business owes to third parties, for example amounts owed to suppliers, bank overdrafts, loans, etc.

Capital is the investment in the business made by the owner. It comprises the initial investment plus profits made, less profits withdrawn by the owner in the form of **drawings**.

If you wish to increase the value of an account with a debit balance or reduce the value of an account with a credit balance, then that account should be debited.

If you wish to increase the value of an account with a credit balance or reduce the value of an account with a debit balance, then that account should be credited.

Illustration

Examples of debit and credit entries

1 Andrew purchases new machinery for his business paying £900 by cheque.

Key terms

DEAD CLIC: a mnemonic to help remember the rules of Debit and Credit
Debit
Expenditure
Assets
Drawings
Credit
Liabilities
Income
Capital.

Assets: resources that are available for use by the business.

Liabilities: monies owed by the business.

Capital: resources (cash or other assets) introduced by the owner to run the business.

Drawings: funds withdrawn from the business by the owner for personal use.

Background knowledge

The accounting equation is a very important principle. You should remember this throughout your studies in accounting as it will apply to every set of financial statements you prepare.

Case study

Norman & Company

Norman & Company was set up in July 2007 by Harry and Christina Norman. They sell books from a rented shop in Canterbury.

AQA Examiner's tip

Take each of the above transactions in turn and decide which two accounts are affected and what effect the transaction will have on those accounts. It will help if you undertake this exercise by reference to the mnemonic 'DEAD CLIC'.

Debit	Credit	Explanation
Machinery		New machinery is an asset, so the value of the asset of machinery increases by £900
	Bank	The value of the asset of cash in the bank decreases by £900

2 Brian sells goods for £400 cash.

Debit	Credit	Explanation
Cash		Cash is an asset, so the value of cash increases by £400
	Sales	At the same time, income increases by £400

3 Christine pays £800 rent by cheque.

Debit	Credit	Explanation
Rent		Expenditure is a debit
	Bank	Cash at bank is an asset, so the value of cash at bank reduces by £800

Illustration

How to detail double entry

Norman & Company sells books. The following transactions were recorded in the first week of trading.

1 July	Introduced capital of £10,000 into the bank account.
2 July	Purchased a delivery van for £2,500 paying by cheque.
3 July	Purchased books for resale on credit from Bookworm Ltd for £4,300.
3 July	Sold books for £540. Customer paid by cheque.
3 July	Sold books for £2,280 on credit to Daly Bookshops.
4 July	Purchased books for resale £580 paying by cheque.
6 July	Paid rent by cheque £1,200.
7 July	Paid cheque for £600 for drawings.

Required

Detail the double entry for each of the above transactions.

Date	Solution	Explanation
1 July	Dr Cash at bank	Cash at bank is an asset and it increases by £10,000.
	Cr Capital	Capital is the cash introduced into the business and this increases the balance of capital.
2 July	Dr Delivery van	Delivery van is an asset and this increases with the purchase.
	Cr Cash at bank	Cash at bank is also an asset, but this decreases when the van is paid for.
3 July	Dr Purchases	Purchases are expenditure for the business and purchases increase.
	Cr Creditors	Creditors are a liability (a credit) and these also increase.
3 July	Dr Cash at bank	Cash at bank is an asset and it increases by £540.
	Cr Sales	Sales are income (a credit) and these also increase by £540.

3 July	Dr Debtors	Debtors are assets, money owed to the business, and these increase.
	Cr Sales	Sales are income (a credit) and these also increase.
4 July	Dr Purchases	Purchases are expenditure for the business and purchases increase.
	Cr Cash at bank	Cash at bank is also an asset, but this decreases when the books are paid for.
6 July	Dr Rent	Rent is expenditure for the business and the charge for rent increases.
	Cr Cash at bank	Cash at bank is also an asset, but this decreases when the rent is paid.
7 July	Dr Drawings	Drawings are expenditure by the business and these increase.
	Cr Cash at bank	Cash at bank is an asset and this decreases when the cheque for drawings is paid.

Stages in the accounting process

The flow chart in Figure 2.3 shows the stages in the accounting process following a transaction through the records.

The role of different source documents

Invoices

The seller of goods or services provides an **invoice** for the buyer. This invoice will detail the following information:

- *Addresses* – the supplier's address, the customer's address and the delivery address (if different).
- *Dates* – the order date and the delivery date.
- *Reference* – a unique invoice number will be present, together with the customer's order number.
- *Description* of the goods or services supplied.
- *Value* – the total amount owed by the customer.
- *Terms* – when the invoice is due for payment and any discount that is available to the customer.

The invoice informs the buyer how much is being paid for the goods or services.

Credit notes

Credit notes are sent from the supplier to the customer when an adjustment to the amount owed is required. This may for example, be due to a calculation error, an incorrect delivery, damage to the goods, returned goods or goods lost in transit.

The details to be included on a credit note are identical to those found on an invoice.

The credit note informs the buyer how much has been deducted from the amount owed to the supplier.

Cheque counterfoils

When a cheque is written, the details are recorded on the **cheque counterfoil** and this becomes the source document.

Key terms

Invoice: a document detailing the goods or services supplied and the price paid.

Source documents

Invoices, credit notes, cheque counterfoils, paying-in slip counterfoils, cash receipts, till rolls, information from bank statements

↓

Books of original entry

General journal, day books, cash book

↓

Ledgers

Sales ledger, purchase ledger, general ledger (nominal ledger)

↓

Trial balance

Extracted from the general ledger

↓

Final accounts

Trading account, profit and loss account, balance sheet

Figure 2.3 *Accounting process*

The details to be recorded are:

- the date of the cheque
- the payee (the person the cheque is made payable to)
- the amount of the cheque
- each cheque has a unique sequential number and this must be included when the details are transferred into the accounting records.

Paying-in slip counterfoils

When cash or cheques are paid into the bank, the details are recorded on the **paying-in slip counterfoil** and this becomes the source document.

The details to be recorded are:

- the date of the paying-in
- the drawers of cheques (the persons paying the organisation) or the source of cash banked
- the amount of the cheques/cash banked.

Cash receipts and till rolls

When cash or cheques are received by a business, a **cash receipt** will be issued. This receipt may take the form of a till roll or alternatively may be a hand-written receipt. The duplicate copies of these receipts form the source document for cash and cheque receipts.

Information from bank statements

Payments and receipts may be debited or credited directly through the bank account. In these circumstances the **bank statement** itself becomes the source document for

- **Direct debits.** Where authority is granted by the business to a third party (for example a supplier of goods or services) for fixed or variable payments to be made at the request of that third party.
- **Standing orders.** Where a fixed payment is made at regular intervals by the bank on the instructions of the business.
- **Bank interest and charges.** Where the bank processes its charge to the business for maintenance of the bank account or the interest on funds borrowed or invested.
- **Credit transfers.** Where money has been paid direct into the bank account of the business by a third party.

Petty cash vouchers

When small payments are made by cash, a **petty cash voucher** should be made out detailing the date, the amount and what the payment was in respect of. This voucher should be signed by an authorised person and wherever possible should have a receipt attached to it.

Other key documents

Delivery note

A document detailing the goods that have been delivered by the supplier. This should be signed by the recipient and a copy returned to the supplier as proof of delivery.

Purchase order

A document raised by the purchasing department used to place an order with a supplier.

Remittance advice

A document sent with a payment advising the recipient which invoices, etc. are being paid.

Statement of account

A document sent to a customer detailing all recent transactions and informing them of the total amount outstanding.

Activity

Source documents

1 Explain the purpose of source documents.

2 Identify the source document that would provide information to enter in the accounting records in each of the following cases.

Transaction	Source document
Direct debit payment for rent.	
Cash paid into the bank.	
Goods purchased on credit from a supplier.	
Credit for goods returned from a customer.	
Cheque paid to a supplier.	
Credit transfer receipt from a customer.	
Cash payment to the window cleaner.	
Goods sold to a customer on credit.	

Key terms

Bank statement: a printout issued by the bank detailing all receipts into the account, payments out of the account and a running balance.

Direct debit: where authority is granted by the business to a third party for fixed or variable payments to be made at the request of that third party.

Standing order: where a fixed payment is made at regular intervals by the bank on the instructions of the business.

Petty cash voucher: contains details of small cash payments made.

Delivery note: a document detailing the goods that have been delivered by the supplier.

Purchase order: a document used to place an order with a supplier.

Remittance advice: a document sent with a payment, advising the recipient which invoices, etc. are being paid.

Statement of account: a document sent to a customer detailing all recent transactions and informing them of the total amount outstanding.

Learning outcomes

As a result of studying this topic, you should now be able to:

- recognise the source documents and identify their purpose
- understand the operation of double entry bookkeeping principles
- account for basic cash and cheque transactions in a double entry bookkeeping system

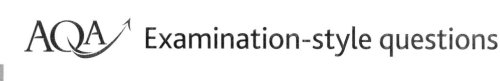

AQA Examination-style questions

1 State two examples of an asset and two examples of a liability.

2 Explain the purpose of a cheque counterfoil and a paying-in counterfoil.

2　Subsidiary books

In this topic you will learn:

- how to account for source documents in the subsidiary books.

Background knowledge

The subsidiary books are sometimes referred to as the books of prime entry – the first point of entry into the records of the business.

Key terms

Sales day book: book of original entry recording credit sales invoices.

General ledger: a ledger containing all impersonal accounts (those accounts that are not customers or suppliers).

Background knowledge

The subsidiary books are where transactions are recorded from the source documents described in Topic 1. The main books are as follows.

- Sales day book
- Sales returns day book
- Purchases returns day book
- Purchases returns day book
- Cash book

💡 Sales day book

The **sales day book** is simply a list of all credit sales transactions. Depending on the volume of transactions, the sales day book will be totalled daily, weekly or monthly. The usual layout for the sales day book is as follows:

Date	Customer	Total (£)
1 May	ABC Ltd	176.25
2 May	DEF Ltd	258.50
		434.75

Figure 2.4 *Sales day book*

Note

The individual total of the invoice will be posted to the debit of the customer's account in the sales ledger. The individual customer accounts in the sales ledger form part of the double entry system. The double entry is completed by posting the total amount to Sales in the **general ledger**.

The double entry postings in the above sales day book example are:

DEBIT ABC Ltd £176.25						
DEBIT DEF Ltd £258.50						
CREDIT Sales account £434.75						
Dr			Sales account			Cr
Date	Details	£	Date	Details		£
			2 May	Sales day book		434.75

Figure 2.5 *Double entry postings*

The customers' accounts in the sales ledger will appear as follows (see Figure 2.6), reflecting the amount owed (debtors) by these two companies.

Dr			ABC Ltd		Cr
Date	Details	£	Date	Details	£
1 May	Sales day book	176.25			
Dr			DEF Ltd		Cr
Date	Details	£	Date	Details	£
2 May	Sales day book	258.50			

Figure 2.6 *Customer accounts*

Sales returns day book

The **sales returns day book** is a list of all credit notes issued to customers. The usual layout for the sales returns day book is identical to the sales day book shown above. As was the case with the sales day book, the individual total of the credit note will be posted this time to the credit of the customer's account in the sales ledger and the total amount of credit notes will be posted to the DEBIT of Sales Returns account in the general ledger.

Key terms

Sales returns day book: book of original entry recording sales credit notes.

Purchases day book

The **purchases day book** is a list of all supplier invoices received in respect of credit transactions. As is the case with the sales day book, depending on the volume of transactions, this will also be totalled daily, weekly or monthly. The usual layout for the purchases day book is identical to the sales day book.

Purchases Day Book		
Date	Supplier	Gross (£)
1 June	PQR Ltd	98.70
2 June	STU Ltd	705.00
		803.70

Figure 2.7 *Purchases day book*

Background knowledge

Sales returns are often referred to as returns inwards.

Note

As was the case with the sales day book, the individual total of the invoice will this time be posted to the credit of the supplier's account in the purchase ledger. The individual supplier accounts in the purchases ledger form part of the double entry system. The double entry (see Figure 2.8) is completed by posting the total amount to Purchases in the general ledger.

The double entry postings in the above example are:					
DEBIT Purchases £803.70					
CREDIT PQR Ltd £98.70					
CREDIT STU Ltd £705.00					
Dr		Purchases account			Cr
Date	Details	£	Date	Details	£
2 June	Purchases day book	803.70			

Figure 2.8 *Double entry postings*

The suppliers' accounts in the sales ledger will now appear as follows, reflecting the amount owing (creditors) to these two companies**.**

Dr					PQR Ltd		Cr
Date	Details		£	Date	Details		£
				1 June	Purchase day book		98.70

Dr					STU Ltd		Cr
Date	Details		£	Date	Details		£
				2 June	Purchase day book		705.00

Figure 2.9 *Supplier's accounts in the sales ledger*

Purchases returns day book

The **purchases returns day book** is a list of all credit notes received from suppliers. The usual layout for the purchases returns day book is identical to the purchases day book shown above. As was the case with the purchases day book, the individual total of the credit note will be posted this time to the debit of the supplier's account in the purchases ledger and the total amount of credit notes will be posted to the CREDIT of Purchases Returns account in the general ledger.

Analysed sales/purchase day book

An analysed day book (see Figure 2.10) would be used when the organisation required more analysis of their **sales** or **purchases**. This analysis could be for different products, different expense headings, different locations, etc. The double entry process is identical to that employed with a traditional day book, though postings of the analysed columns would be into different accounts in the general ledger dependent upon the analysis.

Date	Supplier	Total (£)	Purchases	Rent & rates	Advertising	Office costs	Other expenses

Figure 2.10 *Purchase day book*

Activity

Day books

Enter the following into the relevant day books.

1. Invoice for £312 sent to customer Farrow on 3 August.
2. Invoice dated 5 August for goods purchased from Blake Hardware for £883.
3. Credit note for goods to the value of £55 retuned from customer Farrow dated 8 August.
4. Invoice for £175 goods purchased from Davies & Co on 9 August.
5. Goods returned to Blake Hardware on 12 August to the value of £102.
6. Goods sold to Campbell Ltd for £1,725 on 15 August.
7. Goods sent to Farrow on 15 August to the value of £322.
8. £122 goods returned by Campbell Ltd on 19 August.

Sales Day Book

Date	Customer		Total (£)

Purchase Day Book

Date	Supplier		Total (£)

Sales Returns Day Book

Date	Customer		Total (£)

Purchase Returns Day Book

Date	Supplier		Total (£)

Cash Book

The cash book records all cash and bank transactions, together with details of discount allowed and discount received.

Whilst there are a variety of acceptable formats for a cash book (including analysed), the most common presentation is as follows:

Background knowledge

The three-column cash book records all movements in and out of the bank and cash together with details of discounts allowed and received.

Dr						Cash Book				Cr
Date	Details	Discount allowed	Cash	Bank	Date	Details received	Discount	Cash	Bank

Figure 2.11 *Cash book*

The following table will help you remember into which side of the cash book data is to be entered.

Table 2.1 *Cash book data*

Cash columns	
Debit	**Credit**
Opening balance – cash in hand	
Cash received	Cash paid
Cheque drawn for cash	
	Closing balance – cash in hand

Bank columns	
Debit	**Credit**
Opening balance – cash in bank	Opening balance – bank overdraft
Cheques received	Cheques paid
Bank interest received	Bank interest and charges paid
Credit transfers	Direct debits and standing orders paid
	Cheque drawn for cash
Closing balance – bank overdraft	Closing balance – cash in bank

Examiner's tip

Don't forget, when a cheque is drawn for cash it will appear on both sides of the cash book. Debit the cash column and credit the bank column.

Activity

Cash book entries

State the entries that would appear in the cash book for the following transactions:

1 On 2 October paid a cheque for £135 to H Ahmed after taking £15 discount.

2 On 3 October withdrew cash from the bank of £50.

3 On 4 October received a cheque for £405 from R Wilkins having allowed discount of £45.

Balancing and closing off the cash book

At the end of the period, the **cash book** should be balanced and closed off.

1 Total all three debit column and all three credit columns.

2 To balance the cash column, enter the balancing figure in the side with the smaller total and label this 'Balance c/d' and date the final day of the accounting period. This balance is then transferred to the opposite side of the cash book as the opening balance. This should be labelled 'Balance b/d' and dated the first day of the next accounting period – see illustration below.

3 The totals of the discount allowed column and the discount received column are the final totals. These will eventually be posted to the general ledger to complete the double entry.

4 Exactly the same process should be carried out on the bank column to ascertain the bank balance.

Illustration

How to balance and close off the cash book

Dr					Cash Book					Cr
Date	Details	Discount allowed	Cash	Bank	Date	Details	Discount received	Cash	Bank
1 May	Green	48		988	2 May	Smith	22		276
3 May	Brown		84		3 May	Wages		116	
3 May	Bank		200		3 May	Jones			307
5 May	Black	26		342	3 May	Cash			200
					5 May	Abdul	8		106
					5 May	Balance c/d		168	441
		74	284	1,330			30	284	1,330
6 May	Balance b/d		168	441					

As you will see, the discount allowed column and discount received column are totalled, but the balance is NOT carried down. These totals are posted directly to the general ledger as follows:

Dr	Discount allowed account				Cr
Date	Details	£	Date	Details	£
6 May	Cash book	74			

Dr	Discount received account				Cr
Date	Details	£	Date	Details	£
			6 May	Cash book	30

Figure 2.12 *Discount allowed and received*

Note

It is important to recognise the difference between **cash discount** and **trade discount**.

Cash discount

Cash discount is a reduction in the amount owing to a supplier in return for settling their bills early. For example, a customer may be offered

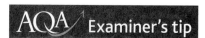

■ **Key terms**

Cash discount: a reduction in the amount owing to a supplier in return for settling their bills early (for example payment within 14 days).

Trade discount: offered to businesses in a similar line of business, as distinct from the general public, often as an incentive for buying in bulk quantities.

Discount received: discount we receive from suppliers for settling our bills promptly.

Discount allowed: discount we give to customers who settle their bills promptly.

■ **Case study**

Potter's Plants

Leon Potter set up his successful gardening business in 1989. He started selling small potting plants from his small garden and due to demand moved his business to larger premises in 1992, where he expanded and started to sell gardening equipment. He now employs 2 other full-time employees and 7 part-time employees.

2% discount if the bill is settled within 14 days. The customer has the choice of taking the discount if settled within the specified terms, or alternatively settling outside the terms and paying the full amount.

Cash discount is recorded separately in the cash book when the payment or receipt is processed.

Discount received is the discount taken when the business pays its supplier early.

Discount allowed is the discount allowed to a customer for early settlement of a sales invoice.

Trade discount

Trade discount is offered to businesses in a similar line of business, as distinct from the general public, often as an incentive for buying in bulk quantities.

Trade discount is NOT recorded separately in the books of account; it is simply a reduction of the net price of the goods or services supplied.

■ **Activity**

Sales day book

Enter the following invoices into the sales day book of Thompson Traders:

Invoice 2755	Tate Appliances	£345	No discount offered
Invoice 2756	H Parry	£1,460	Trade discount of 15%
Invoice 2757	D Lane & Co	£720	Cash discount of 5%

■ **Illustration**

How to record information in a cash book and balance it

Leon Potter maintains a manual set of books and the following transactions took place during the week ending 9 April.

4 April	Balances brought forward – cash in hand £53, bank overdraft £13,582.
4 April	Cash sales £312
5 April	Cheque paid to G Spooner £440 (discount taken £18)
5 April	Bank interest paid £128
6 April	Cheque received from Baird Ltd £89
8 April	Cheque drawn for petty cash £900
8 April	Paid wages by cash £617
9 April	Cheque received from Lord & Co £5,238 (discount allowed £214)
9 April	Cash paid into the bank £312

Required

Record this information in the cash book below and balance the cash book at 10 April.

Dr					Cash Book					Cr
Date	Details	Discount allowed	Cash	Bank	Date	Details	Discount received	Cash	Bank	

Explanations

Date	Transaction	Explanation
4 April	Balances brought forward – cash in hand £53, bank overdraft £13,582	The balance of cash brought forward is in hand and therefore an asset and a debit balance. The bank is overdrawn and therefore a liability and a credit balance.
4 April	Cash sales £312	Cash received will increase the asset of cash – debit cash.
5 April	Cheque paid to G Spooner £440 (discount taken £18)	Cheque paid will increase the overdraft, therefore credit bank. The discount of £18 is analysed into the discount received column.
5 April	Bank interest paid £128	Bank interest paid will increase the bank overdraft – credit bank.
6 April	Cheque received from Baird Ltd £89	The cheque received will reduce the overdraft – debit bank.
8 April	Cheque drawn for petty cash £900	The cheque drawn for cash affects both the cash column and the bank column. The asset of cash is increased – debit cash. The liability of bank overdraft is also increased – credit bank.
8 April	Paid wages by cash £617	The wages paid will reduce the cash balance – credit cash.
9 April	Cheque received from Lord & Co £5,238 (discount allowed £214)	Cheque received will reduce the bank overdraft – debit bank. The discount of £214 will be analysed into the discount allowed column.
9 April	Cash paid into the bank £312	Cash banked will reduce the bank overdraft – debit bank. It will also reduce the balance of cash in hand – credit cash.

Solution

Dr					Cash Book				Cr
Date	Details	Discount allowed	Cash	Bank	Date	Details	Discount received	Cash	Bank
4 Apr	Balance b/d		53		4 Apr	Balance b/d			13,582
4 Apr	Cash sales		312		5 Apr	G Spooner	18		440
6 Apr	Baird Ltd			89	5 Apr	Bank Interest			128
8 Apr	Bank		900		8 Apr	Cash			900
9 Apr	Lord & Co	214		5,238	8 Apr	Wages		617	
9 Apr	Cash			312	9 Apr	Bank		312	
9 Apr	Balance c/d			9,411	9 Apr	Balance c/d		336	
		214	1,265	15,050			18	1,265	15,050
10 Apr	Balance b/d		336		10 Apr	Balance b/d			9,411

The general journal

The **general journal** is a book of original entry – a subsidiary book. The journal is used to record non-routine transactions or entries when no other book of original entry is suitable.

The journal will be used for:

- The correction of errors.
- Transferring amounts from one general ledger account to another.
- Processing the entry for depreciation.
- The purchase or sale of fixed assets.

Why is the journal necessary?

- It reduces the risk of fraud. The journal forms an integral part of the audit trail and as such reduces the possibility of unauthorised transactions being entered in the accounting records.
- It reduces the risk of incorrect entries by detailing the transactions as they are to be entered in the accounting records.
- It provides a permanent record of non-routine transactions entered in the accounting records.

The format of the journal

The journal is set out as follows:

Date	Details	Dr (£)	Cr (£)
30 June	Motor vehicle cost	4,500	
	Motor expenses		4,500
	Correction of posting error		

Figure 2.13 *Journal*

Note that it is good practice to provide a short narrative giving details of what the entry relates to.

Key terms

General journal: book of original entry recording non-routine transactions that do not appear in the other books of original entry.

Background knowledge

Remember, the journal is not part of double entry bookkeeping – it is a subsidiary book listing transactions before they are entered into the accounts.

Activity

General journal

Show the journal entries necessary to correct the following two errors

1 £110 cash received for sales has been incorrectly posted to the credit of purchases.

2 £415 paid for rent has been incorrectly posted to repairs.

Case study

Trent Gallery

On 1 October 2007, Brian Trent started his own business. He is an artist in his spare time and decided to open a small art gallery selling his own paintings and those of other local artists. Brian has an electronic cash register, but maintains a manual set of accounting records.

During the first week of trading, the following transactions took place and he was able to identify the source documents and the subsidiary books that had to be used to record them.

Transaction	Source document	Subsidiary book
Introduced capital of £20,000 into the bank account	Bank paying-in book	Cash book
Withdrew £500 cash from the bank	Cheque counterfoil	Cash book
Bought £1,300 paintings for resale on credit from Tony Jones	Purchase invoice	Purchases day book
Paid window cleaner £13 by cash	Petty cash voucher	Cash book
Cash sales of £65	Till roll	Cash book
Bought goods for resale £368 from Gold Ltd	Purchase invoice	Purchases day book
Paid £120 into the bank	Bank paying-in book	Cash book
Sold goods to Ellison for £800 on credit	Sales invoice	Sales day book
Received a credit note for damaged goods returned to Gold Ltd £33	Purchase credit note	Purchases day book
Received a cheque for £800 from Ellison and paid this into the bank	Bank paying-in book	Cash book

Learning outcomes

As a result of studying this topic, you should now be able to:

- explain the purpose of the day books
- explain the process of posting entries from the day books into the ledgers
- explain the purpose and structure of the cash book
- explain the difference between cash discount and trade discount
- explain the purpose of the general journal

 Examination-style questions

1 ACC1, June 2001

Complete the grid by stating which document and subsidiary book (or book of prime entry) would be used for each of the following transactions.

	Transaction	Document	Subsidiary Book (or book of prime entry)
(a)	Selling goods on credit to a customer		

(b)	Reducing the price charged to the customer		
(c)	Banking the payment made by the customer		
(d)	Refund made to the customer		

2 Explain the difference between cash discount and trade discount. How does the treatment of these differ in the accounting records?

3 Excel Marketing is a marketing and promotions business, maintaining a three-column cash book. The balances in the cash book at 1 May 2008 were as follows:

Cash   £341 Debit

Bank   £1,956 Credit

The following are details of transactions that took place in the first week of May:

		£
1 May	Received cheque from Alan Levy in full settlement of debt of £675	650
2 May	Paid for petrol by cash	46
2 May	Paid Harvey Ltd by cheque	711
3 May	Banked sales receipts	286
4 May	Paid Paul Dann by cheque, taking £31 discount	917
4 May	Withdrew cash from the bank	600
4 May	Paid wages by cash	614
4 May	Paid salaries by cheque	1,486
5 May	Introduced capital into the bank account	2,000
5 May	Paid deposit on new machinery by cheque	500
6 May	Paid insurance by direct debit	51
6 May	Received cheque from Ashby Ltd (discount £43)	857
6 May	Received cheque from XT Motors in full settlement of debt of £1,783	1,700
7 May	Paid rates by cheque	926

Required

Enter the transactions in the cash book. Balance the cash and bank columns carrying down the balances at 8 May and total the discount columns.

3   Ledger accounts

In this topic you will learn:

■ how to post transactions from subsidiary books into ledgers

■ how to balance and close off accounts.

Periodically, the subsidiary books will be totalled and the totals will be transferred into the ledger system.

Ledgers are an essential part of the double entry bookkeeping system, containing all of the information grouped together for a specific customer, supplier or general ledger account.

Sales ledger

The **sales ledger** contains personal accounts for each individual customer to whom we sell goods or provide services on a credit basis as distinct from a cash sale basis. The account summarises all transactions with a particular customer and shows what they owe the business. A typical sales ledger account will contain some or all of the items detailed below.

Dr	Green & Co					Cr
Date	Details	£	Date	Details		£
1 Nov	Balance b/d	5,425	30 Nov	Bank		9,780
30 Nov	Sales day book	11,653	30 Nov	Discounts allowed		236
30 Nov	**Returned cheques**	112	30 Nov	Sales returns day book		270
			30 Nov	**Contras**		340
			30 Nov	**Bad debts written off**		50
			30 Nov	Balance c/d		6,514
		17,190				17,190
1 June	Balance b/d	6,514				

Figure 2.14 *Sales ledger*

Key terms

Sales ledger: a ledger containing individual personal accounts for each credit customer and recording all transactions with that customer.

Bad debt written off: amount owed by a debtor that is irrecoverable.

Contra: an amount set off in the sales ledger account against the purchases ledger account of the same person(s).

Returned cheque: a cheque that has been paid into the bank, but not honoured by the drawer's bank (usually because of lack of funds).

Note that the account commences with the balance brought down at the start of the period as a debit balance since customers who owe the business money are debtors.

As you will see later, the sales ledger control account mirrors each individual personal account, but is a total account including all transactions that are posted to all of the customer accounts.

Purchase ledger

The **purchase ledger** (see Figure 2.15) contains personal accounts for each individual supplier from whom we purchase goods or services on a credit basis as distinct from a cash sale basis. The account summarises all transactions with a particular supplier and shows what the business owes to them. A typical purchase ledger account will contain some or all of the items detailed below.

Key terms

Purchase ledger: a ledger containing individual personal accounts for each credit supplier and recording all transactions with that supplier.

Dr	Brown & Co				Cr
Date	Details	£	Date	Details	£
30 Nov	Bank	6,411	1 Nov	Balance b/d	3,440
30 Nov	Discounts received	58	30 Nov	Purchases day book	5,285
30 Nov	Purchases returns day book	108	30 Nov	Cancelled cheques	312
30 Nov	Contras	213			
30 Nov	Balance c/d	2,247			
		9,037			9,037
			1 Dec	Balance b/d	2,247

Figure 2.15 *Purchase ledger*

Note that the account commences with the balance brought down at the start of the period as a credit balance since suppliers to whom the business money owes are creditors.

As you will see later, the purchase ledger control account mirrors each individual personal account, but is a total account including *all* transactions that are posted to *all* of the supplier accounts.

Balancing and closing off personal ledger accounts

Periodically, all ledger accounts are balanced and closed off. This process involves totalling both sides of the account and entering the balancing figure in the side with the smaller total to enable the account to balance. This balancing figure is then carried down on the opposite side as the commencing figure for the next accounting period.

Example 1 – debit and credit column totals are the same

In this example, since both totals are identical, the account is totalled and ruled off.

Dr			A Smith			Cr
Date	Details	£	Date	Details		£
1 Nov	Balance b/d	3,200	30 Nov	Bank		7,360
30 Nov	Sales day book	4,160				
		7,360				7,360

Figure 2.16 *Example 1*

Example 2 – debit and credit column totals are not equal

In this example, the totals of the debit and credit columns are not equal, so the difference between the two columns (£9,630) is entered on the credit side to balance the account and is carried down on the debit side as the opening balance for the next accounting period.

Dr			A Jones		Cr
Date	Details	£	Date	Details	£
1 Nov	Balance b/d	2,480	30 Nov	Bank	4,500
30 Nov	Sales day book	11,650	30 Nov	Balance c/d	9,630
		14,130			14,130
1 Dec	Balance b/d	9,630			

Figure 2.17 *Example 2*

Activity

Balancing sales ledger account

Balance the following sales ledger account for Williams & Co

Dr			Williams & Co		Cr
Date	Details	£	Date	Details	£
1 Feb	Balance b/d	17,536	28 Feb	Sales returns day book	512
28 Feb	Sales day book	62,508	28 Feb	Bank	61,227
			28 Feb	Discount allowed	533
			28 Feb	Contra	300

General ledger

The **general ledger** contains all of the remaining impersonal accounts. Impersonal accounts are those accounts that do relate to a person or another business and these are either

- **real accounts**, which record fixed assets, for example machinery or motor vehicles, or
- **nominal accounts**, which record revenue and expense items, for example sales, purchases, stationery, etc.
- The balances from the general ledger form the basis of the trial balance.

Balancing and closing off general ledger accounts

The process of **balancing off** and closing off general ledger accounts depends on the nature of the account.

Example 1 – trading account

A trading account item such as sales, purchases, carriage inwards, etc. will be closed off by transfer to the trading account.

Dr			Sales			Cr
Date	Details	£	Date	Details		£
30 Nov	*Trading account*	**88,949**	30 Nov	Sales day book		86,467
			30 Nov	Bank		2,482
		88,949				88,949

Figure 2.18 *Trading account*

Example 2 – profit and loss account

A profit and loss account item such as discount allowed, stationery, etc. will be closed off by transfer to the profit and loss account.

Dr			Stationery		Cr
Date	Details	£	Date	Details	£
30 Nov	Purchase day book	2,144	*30 Nov*	*Profit and loss account*	**2,282**
30 Nov	Bank	138			
		2,282			2,282

Figure 2.19 *Profit and loss account*

Example 3 – balance sheet

A balance sheet item such as machinery or cash at bank will be closed off by carrying the balance down to the start of the next accounting period.

Dr			Machinery		Cr
Date	Details	£	Date	Details	£
1 Nov	Balance b/d	18,450	*30 Nov*	*Balance c/d*	**19,810**
30 Nov	Journal	1,360			
		19,810			19,810
1 Dec	*Balance b/d*	**19,810**			

Figure 2.20 *Balance sheet*

Key terms

General ledger: a ledger containing all impersonal accounts.

Real accounts: a type of impersonal account relating to fixed assets.

Nominal accounts: a type of impersonal account relating to all non-real accounts.

Background knowledge

Periodic balancing and closing off of ledger accounts keeps the ledger much tidier and easier to read.

¹₂₃ ✓ Illustration

How to balance and close off the cashbook

The following transactions took place at Khan Kitchens during the first week of May.

All sales and purchases are made on credit.

1 May	Purchased goods from Byfield Ltd for £430.
3 May	Purchased goods from Lee Units for £2,795.
3 May	Sold goods to Garside Kitchens for £978.
3 May	Purchased goods from BM Modules £3,570.
4 May	Received a credit note from Lee Units for £322.
4 May	Sold goods to H Brunning for £1,880.
5 May	Sold goods to Malcolm & Co for £3,094.
5 May	Sent a credit note to Garside Kitchens for £85.
5 May	Purchased goods from Byfield Ltd for £5,337.
6 May	Sold goods to Garside Kitchens for £2,680

Required

Enter the above transactions in the appropriate day books of Khan Kitchens, complete the postings to the purchase ledger, sales ledger and general ledger, and balance and close off all accounts at 7 May.

Approach

- ▨ Ascertain which day books are to be used for each transaction.
- ▨ Post the transactions into the relevant day books.
- ▨ Total the day books.
- ▨ Post the individual items from the day books into the personal accounts in the sales ledger and purchase ledger.
- ▨ Post the totals from the day books into the general ledger.
- ▨ Balance and close off all ledger accounts.

Solution

Sales day book		
Date	Customer	Amount (£)
3 May	Garside Kitchens	978
4 May	H Brunning	1,880
5 May	Malcolm & Co	3,094
6 May	Garside Kitchens	2,680
		8,632

Purchase day book		
Date	Supplier	Amount (£)
1 May	Byfield Ltd	430
3 May	Lee Units	2,795
3 May	BM Modules	3,570
5 May	Byfield Ltd	5,337
		12,132

Sales returns day book

Date	Customer	Amount (£)
5 May	Garside Kitchens	85
		85

Purchase returns day book

Date	Customer	Amount (£)
4 May	Lee Units	322
		322

Sales ledger

Dr				Garside Kitchens	Cr
Date	Details	£	Date	Details	£
3 May	Sales day book	978	5 May	Sales returns day book	85
6 May	Sales day book	2,680	7 May	Balance c/d	3,573
		3,658			3,658
8 May	Balance b/d	3,573			

Dr				H Brunning	Cr
Date	Details	£	Date	Details	£
4 May	Sales day book	1,880	7 May	Balance c/d	1,880
		1,880			1,880
8 May	Balance b/d	1,880			

Dr				Malcolm & Co	Cr
Date	Details	£	Date	Details	£
5 May	Sales day book	3,094	7 May	Balance c/d	3,094
		3,094			3,094
8 May	Balance b/d	3,094			

Purchase ledger

Dr				Byfield Ltd	Cr
Date	Details	£	Date	Details	£
7 May	Balance c/d	5,767	1 May	Purchase day book	430
			5 May	Purchase day book	5,337
		5,767			5,767
			8 May	Balance b/d	5,767

Dr			Lee Units			Cr
Date	Details	£	Date	Details		£
4 May	Purchase returns day book	322	3 May	Purchase day book		2,795
7 May	Balance c/d	2,473				
		2,795				2,795
			8 May	Balance b/d		2,473

Dr			BM Modules			Cr
Date	Details	£	Date	Details		£
7 May	Balance c/d	3,570	3 May	Purchase day book		3,570
		3,570				3,570
			8 May	Balance b/d		3,570

Link

For more information on ledger accounts, see Chapter 7, page 88.

General ledger

Dr			Sales			Cr
Date	Details	£	Date	Details		£
7 May	Trading account	8,632	7 May	Sales day book		8,632
		8,632				8,632

Dr			Sales returns			Cr
Date	Details	£	Date	Details		£
7 May	Sales returns day book	85	7 May	Trading account		85
		85				85

Dr			Purchases			Cr
Date	Details	£	Date	Details		£
7 May	Purchase day book	12,132	7 May	Trading account		12,132
		12,132				12,132

Dr			Purchase returns			Cr
Date	Details	£	Date	Details		£
7 May	Trading account	322	3 May	Purchase returns day book		322
		322				322

✓🔲 *Learning outcomes*

As a result of studying this topic, you should now be able to:

■ post transactions from the subsidiary books to the sales ledger and purchase ledger

■ balance and close off personal accounts in the sales ledger and purchase ledger

■ balance and close off general ledger accounts

AQA Examination-style questions

1 The totals of the discount columns in a three-column cash book are as follows

Discount allowed   £634
Discount received   £388

Transfer these totals into the correct general ledger accounts.

2 At 1 June 2008, Garry Parker owed Franklyn Graphics £897.

On 12 June 2008, Garry Parker sent a cheque to Franklyn Graphics for the total amount outstanding at that date after deducting discount of £45.

On 13 June 2008, Franklyn Graphics invoiced Garry Parker for work completed to the value of £595.

On 22 June 2008, Franklyn Graphics sent a credit note to Garry Parker for £113.

Required

Enter the above transactions in the ledger accounts books of Franklyn Graphics. Balance and close off the accounts at 30 June 2008.

3 Verification of accounting records

In the previous chapter, you have learned how to account for a range of transactions from source document, through subsidiary books into the ledger system. This chapter builds on that knowledge by looking at various aspects of verification of the accounting records.

Having processed transactions into the accounting records, we now need to verify the accuracy of the records and the following techniques enable this to be done

- Trial balance to check the arithmetical accuracy of the general ledger.
- Sales and purchases ledger control accounts to check the arithmetical accuracy of the sales and purchases ledgers.
- Bank reconciliation statements to check the arithmetical accuracy of the cash book when compared to the bank statement.
- It is important to recognise that these techniques are checking the arithmetical accuracy – they do not of course guarantee that everything has been posted into the correct account.
- As a result, we shall look at different types of errors, how to correct errors that are revealed and what effect those errors may have on both the trial balance and the profit and loss account.
- It is important to not only be able to prepare trial balances, control accounts and bank reconciliation statements, but you must also be aware of the benefits and limitations of these techniques and be prepared to answer written questions on this subject area.

1 Trial balance

In this topic you will learn:

- to understand the role, presentation and limitations of the trial balance

- how to identify and correct different types of errors affecting the trial balance and the effect that errors may have on the calculation of profit.

The trial balance is simply a listing of all the general ledger balances on a given date. As we have already seen, for every debit there must be equal and corresponding credits. Providing the double entry has been accurately carried out, the total of all debits will equal the total of all credits and the trial balance will balance.

☑️🔑 Presentation of the trial balance

A trial balance will be presented as follows

ABC		
Trial balance at 30 June 2008		
Account	Dr (£)	Cr (£)

Figure 3.1 A trial balance

Illustration

How to prepare a trial balance

Chris's bookkeeper has extracted the following list of balances at the financial year end, 31 October 2008 and has asked for a trial balance to be prepared at that date.

	£
Bank overdraft	5,150
Capital account at 1 November 2007	56,900
Carriage inwards	1,750
Carriage outwards	840
Cash in hand	110
Drawings	24,000
Fixtures and fittings at cost	34,200
Mortgage on premises (repayable 2017)	50,000
Motor running expenses	3,370
Motor vehicle at cost	4,200
Premises at cost	85,000
Purchases	92,150
Rent and rates	5,200
Returns inwards	960
Returns outwards	390
Sales	206,370
Stationery and advertising	1,860
Stock at 1 November 2007	54,080
Trade creditors	5,320
Trade debtors	4,210
Wages	12,200

Approach

Work down the list of balances and decide whether they are a debit entry or a credit entry.

Solution

Trial balance at 31 October 2008

	Dr (£)	Cr (£)
Bank overdraft		5,150
Capital account at 1 November 2007		56,900
Carriage inwards	1,750	
Carriage outwards	840	
Cash in hand	110	
Drawings	24,000	
Fixtures and fittings at cost	34,200	
Mortgage on premises (repayable 2017)		50,000
Motor running expenses	3,370	
Motor vehicle at cost	4,200	
Premises at cost	85,000	
Purchases	92,150	
Rent and rates	5,200	
Returns inwards	960	
Returns outwards		390
Sales		206,370
Stationery and advertising	1,860	
Stock at 1 November 2007	54,080	

Trade creditors		5,320
Trade debtors	4,210	
Wages	12,200	
	324,130	324,130

Acivity

Trial balance errors

James has discovered an error in his accounting records. A payment of £7,000 for machinery has been debited to purchases account.

1 Identify the name of this type of error.

2 Explain why the trial balance should still balance.

Background knowledge

It is very important to recognise different types of error. As you will see in this section, some errors do affect the balancing of the trial balance, others do not.

Key terms

Suspense account: a temporary account used to post a difference in the trial balance (i.e. the total of the debit side does not equal the total of the credit side) until such time as the differences are identified.

■☑ Trial balance errors

Although the trial balance shown in the illustration above does balance, it does not necessarily mean that everything has been posted into the correct account or that all of the transactions have been recorded correctly or indeed been recorded at all.

Some errors will affect the trial balance whilst some will not affect the balancing of the trial balance.

Errors that will NOT be revealed by the trial balance

- **Errors of omission.** Where both sides of the transaction, debit and credit, have been omitted from the records.
- **Compensating error.** Where errors on the debit side equal errors on the credit side and they cancel each other out.
- **Error of commission.** Where an amount is posted to an incorrect account of the correct type. For example Andrew Smith account instead of Alf Smith account.
- **Error of principle.** Where an amount is posted to an incorrect class of account. For example, motor repairs (an expense) are posted to motor vehicles (an asset).
- **Error of original entry.** Where an error is made transferring an amount from the source document into the book of original entry.
- **Error of reversal.** Where the account that should have been debited has been credited and the amount that should have been credited has been debited.

Errors that WILL be revealed by the trial balance

- **Transposition errors.** Where, for example, £54 is incorrectly transposed and posted as £45.
- **Addition errors.** In the trial balance itself or in a general ledger account.
- **Posting errors.** Where one side of the transaction is posted to the wrong side of an account.
- **Partial omission error.** Where one side of the transaction is not posted.
- **Unequal posting error.** Where the debit side of the posting does not equal the credit side.

If the trial balance does not balance

Extracting a trial balance immediately verifies the arithmetical accuracy of the ledger. If the trial balance does not balance, until such time as the errors are identified and corrected, the difference may be entered into a **suspense account** to temporarily balance the account.

Errors and suspense accounts

When the reason for errors is discovered, a journal entry should be processed to remove the amount(s) from the suspense account by transfer into the correct account.

Illustration

How to deal with suspense accounts

The trial balance of Michie & Co. contains errors and a suspense account has been opened with a balance of £90 Dr. It is discovered that the difference was caused by a posting error. A cheque for £540 had been posted to motor expenses account as £450.

To correct the error, £90 (£540 – £450) must be removed from suspense account and transferred to motor expenses account, which is where it should have been posted.

The journal entry to correct this will therefore be

Debit	Motor expenses	£90
Credit	Suspense account	£90

Correction of transposition error

As a result of this transfer, the suspense account now has a zero balance and is no longer required and motor expenses account now reflects the correct figure.

Illustration

How to make entries in the suspense account and show the opening balance

Fancy Goods Enterprises is a successful business, but the inexperienced bookkeeper has made a number of errors throughout the year. The trial balance was drawn up as at 31 March 2001 but the totals did not agree and the following errors have been discovered.

1 The purchases account has been overcast by £4,500.

2 The debtors' total includes £650 that has been written off as a bad debt.

3 Discount received of £300 has been entered on the debit of the account.

4 A cheque for £673, payable to Sunshine Products Ltd has been entered in the account of Sunmaster Products in error.

5 The credit balance in the rent payable account has been brought down as £990; it should have been £909.

Required

You have been asked to make any necessary entries in the suspense account to correct these errors, and show the opening balance.

Dr		Suspense account		Cr
Details	£	Details		£

Approach

You are not given the opening balance on the suspense account, so take each of the errors in turn, assessing the effect each will have on the suspense account. Complete the suspense account with all relevant amounts and enter the difference as the opening balance.

1 Purchases must be reduced by £4,500 – credit purchases, debit suspense account.
2 Debtors must be reduced by £650 – credit debtors, debit suspense account.
3 Discount received of £300 has been entered on the debit of the account, whereas it should have been entered to the credit of the account. As a result, the correction has to be for £600 – £300 to cancel the debit entry and another £300 to place the entry on the credit side of discounts received account. Debit suspense account and credit discounts received account with £600.
4 This error must be corrected through the purchase ledger, but since the cheque has been processed through the correct ledger, but an incorrect personal account, this will not affect the suspense account. No entry is necessary.
5 Rent payable must be increased (debited) by £81 – debit rent payable and credit suspense account.

Solution

The completed suspense account will be as follows

Dr	Suspense account		Cr
Details	£	Details	£
Purchases	4,500	Opening balance	5,669
Debtors	650	Rent payable	81
Discount received	600		
	5,750		5,750

AQA Examiner's tip

Remember, only one side of the correcting entry should appear on the suspense account, the corresponding entry appears on the other account affected by the error.

What is the importance of the trial balance?

- It checks the accuracy of the bookkeeping.
- It is the stepping stone to the preparation of final accounts – the trading and profit and loss account and balance sheet.

Assessing the effect of errors on profit

Errors will often affect the calculation of profit. This could apply to errors that do affect the trial balance or, indeed, errors that do not affect the trial balance.

Examination questions may concentrate on the effect that errors have on the calculation of profit and require the calculation of an amended profit.

AQA Examiner's tip

Bear in mind that errors affecting only balance sheet items will not affect profit.

Illustration

How to calculate the net profit

A trainee accountant for Dublin & Co. produced a draft profit and loss account that showed a net profit for the year ended 31 March 2006 of £17,690. Her supervisor subsequently discovered the following errors.

1 The purchase day book had been undercast by £520.

2 The cost of repairs to a delivery van of £450 had been debited to the motor vehicles account.

3 A payment of £500 for insurance had been completely omitted from the accounts.

4 A cheque for £2,300 received from B Harrison, a debtor, had been credited to the account of B Harris.

5 Discount received of £1,300 had been charged as an expense in the profit and loss account.

6 The closing stock had been recorded in the trading account as £3,000. The correct figure was £300.

Required

You are required to calculate the correct net profit. It is important to show clearly whether each adjustment is added, subtracted or has no effect on the profit calculation.

Corrected net profit for the year ended 31 March 2006

	£
Net profit as given	**17,690**
1	
2	
3	
4	
5	
6	
Corrected net profit	

Approach

Take each point in turn and decide firstly whether it has any effect on the profit calculation and secondly what that effect is.

1 The purchase day book had been undercast by £520, so as a result purchases have been understated by the same amount. Increasing purchases will reduce the net profit.

2 The cost of repairs to a delivery van of £450 had been debited to the motor vehicles account. Since motor vehicles are a fixed asset, correcting this error of principle will increase the expenses of delivery van repair and therefore reduce the net profit.

3 Correcting the omission of the payment of £500 for insurance will increase expenses and therefore reduce the net profit.

4 This error of commission must be corrected through the sales ledger, but since the receipt has been processed through the correct ledger, but an incorrect personal account, this will not affect the net profit.

5 Discount received of £1,300 had been charged as an expense in the profit and loss account, but it should be shown as income. Correcting this error will increase the net profit by £2,600. Firstly, £1,300 to cancel the expense and secondly a further £1,300 to process the income.

6 Closing stock has been overstated by £2,700. Since closing stock is subtracted from the cost of sales, £2,700 too much has been taken away. Correcting this error will increase the cost of sales by £2,700 and therefore reduce the net profit.

Solution

Corrected net profit for the year ended 31 March 2006

			£
	Net profit as given		17,690
1	Purchases undercast	Subtract	520
2	Delivery van repairs	Subtract	450
3	Insurance omitted	Subtract	500
4	Error of commission	No effect	
5	Discount received	Add	2,600
6	Closing stock overstated	Subtract	2,700
	Corrected net profit		16,120

 *Learning outcomes*

As a result of studying this topic, you should now be able to:

- state the purpose and importance of the trial balance
- identify errors that both affect and do not affect the trial balance
- correct errors by the use of the suspense account
- assess the effect that errors will have on the calculation of profit

AQA Examination-style questions

1 Detail the sources of information for the trial balance.

2 Brian runs a dry cleaning business. A trial balance at 31 July 2008 has been prepared, but the following balances have not yet been included

	£
Premises at cost	145,000
Mortgage on premises (repayable January 2009)	60,000
Capital	80,000
Carriage inwards	1,060
Carriage outwards	3,422
Drawings	28,525
Returns inwards	612
Returns outwards	1,802

Complete the trial balance below. Enter any difference as 'bank balance'

Account	Dr (£)	Cr (£)
Capital		
Carriage inwards		
Carriage outwards		
Creditors		6,770
Debtors	3,286	
Drawings		

Mortgage on premises (repayable January 2009)		
Motor expenses	11,403	
Premises at cost		
Purchases	31,518	
Rent and rates	32,400	
Returns inwards		
Returns outwards		
Sales		126,380
Stock at 1 August 2007	2,490	
Wages and salaries	23,376	
Bank balance		

3 ACC1 June 2001

(a) What is the source of the figures used to construct the trial balance?

(b) Describe two uses of the trial balance.

(c) Comment on the limitations of trial balances as a means of checking the accuracy of the ledger, Use two examples to illustrate your answer.

4 Adapted from ACC1 June 2003

The trial balance of H G Patel as at 30 April 2003 has been partially completed. The following balances have now to be included:

	£
Purchases	38 900
Sales	98 000
Returns outwards	3 698
Carriage inwards	367
Carriage outwards	450
Discount received	2 135
Drawings	6 900

(a) Complete the trial balance.

(b) Total the trial balance and enter any difference in the suspense account.

H G Patel: Trial balance as at 30 April 2003		
Account	Debit (£)	Credit (£)
Wages	23,890	
Administration costs	6,000	
Capital		60,000
Premises	65,000	
Motor vehicles	5,000	
Motor expenses	1,650	

Purchases		
Sales		
Returns outwards		
Carriage inwards		
Carriage outwards		
Discount received		
Drawings		
Suspense account		
TOTAL		

5   ACC1 January 2002

Northern Lights drew up the following trial balance. When it was totalled it revealed errors which resulted in a suspense account being opened.

Northern Lights		
Trial balance as at 31 December 2001		
	Dr	Cr
Sales		400,000
Purchases	350,000	
Returns inwards		5,000
Returns outwards	6,200	
Stock at 1 January 2001	100,000	
Carriage outwards	800	
Wages	32,000	
Rates	6,000	
Carriage inwards		1,000
Fixed assets		70,000
Debtors		9,800
Creditors	7,000	
Bank balance (overdrawn)	3,000	
Drawings	18,000	
Capital		106,400
Loan from bank	70,000	
Suspense account		800
Total	**593,000**	**593,000**

Draw up the corrected trial balance, using the grid below.

Northern Lights		
Trial balance as at 31 December 2001		
	Dr	Cr
Sales		
Purchases		
Returns inwards		
Returns outwards		
Stock at 1 January 2001		
Carriage outwards		
Wages		
Rates		

Carriage inwards		
Fixed assets		
Debtors		
Creditors		
Bank balance (overdrawn)		
Drawings		
Capital		
Loan from bank		
Suspense account		
Total		

6 ACC1 January 2007

Bill Burgess runs a business selling mobile phones. The trial balance at 31 October 2006 has been partially completed, but the following balances have not yet been included.

	£
Premises	10,400
Debtors	3,610
Creditors	1,870
Capital	10,000
Mortgage on premises	3,000
Drawings	14,400

(a)   Complete the trial balance below.

(b)   Total the trial balance and enter the difference as 'Bank Balance'.

Trial Balance at 31 October 2006

Account	Debit £	Credit £
Sales		57,120
Purchases	18,340	
Stock at 1 November 2005	5,300	
General expenses	8,850	
Wages	12,460	
Motor vehicles	2,000	
Premises		
Debtors		
Creditors		
Capital		
Mortgage on premises		
Drawings		
Bank balance		
Totals		

After completing the trial balance, you are told that a payment of £2,500 for Motor Vehicles had been incorrectly posted to General Expenses.

(c)   State what type of error this is.

(d)   State why the trial balance should still balance.

(e)   Explain with reasons, what effect, if any, this error would have on the profit for the year.

2   Bank reconciliation statement

In this topic you will learn:

- to understand the role, presentation and limitations of the bank reconciliation

- how to produce a bank reconciliation statement.

Background knowledge

Businesses will prepare a bank reconciliation regularly. This enables the early detection of any errors in the cash book, but also acts as a deterrent to fraud.

AQA Examiner's tip

Remember, if the opening balance as per the cash book is overdrawn, unpresented cheques will be **deducted** and outstanding lodgements **added**.

Key terms

Unpresented cheques: cheques that have been drawn and entered in the cash book, but have not yet been presented to the bank for payment.

Outstanding (uncleared) lodgements: bank deposits that have been recorded in the cash book but have not yet been processed by the bank.

Direct debit: where authority is granted by the business to a third party for fixed or variable payments to be made at the request of that third party.

Standing order: where a fixed payment is made at regular intervals by the bank on the instructions of the business.

The purpose of the bank reconciliation statement is to reconcile the balance as per the cash book with the balance as per the bank statement.

In other words, *internal* records (the cash book) can be reconciled with *external* records (the bank statements).

The reasons why these two balances may not agree are:

- **Unpresented cheques**. Cheques drawn but not yet presented for payment through the bank account.
- **Outstanding lodgements**. Cash or cheques paid into the bank that have not yet been recorded on the bank statement.
- Items that have been debited or credited directly to the bank account that have not yet been entered in the cash book (e.g. bank interest or charges, **direct debits**, **standing orders**, etc.).

Bank reconciliation statement – structure

The structure of a bank reconciliation statement is as follows:

Balance as per cash book		XXX
Add: unpresented cheques	XXX	
	XXX	
	XXX	XXX
		XXX
Less: outstanding lodgements	XXX	
	XXX	XXX
Balance as per bank statement		XXX

Figure 3.2 *Bank reconciliation statement*

The bank reconciliation may also be produced commencing with the balance as per the bank statement. In this case, unpresented cheques should be deducted (they will reduce the balance in the bank when they are presented) and outstanding lodgements should be added.

Preparing a bank reconciliation statement

Step 1   Tick all items that appear on the bank statement and also in the cash book.

Step 2   Enter into the cash book any items that appear on the bank statement, but not in the cash book.

Step 3   Balance the bank columns of the cash book and carry down the closing balance.

Step 4   Start the bank reconciliation statement by entering the closing balance as per the cash book.

Step 5   Unticked payments in the cash book are the unpresented cheques. Enter these into the bank reconciliation.

Step 6 Unticked receipts in the cash book are outstanding lodgements. Enter these into the bank reconciliation.

Step 7 Calculate the closing balance on the bank reconciliation statement. This should agree with the balance as per the bank statement.

Remember

- A **bank statement** is a record of the customer's account in the books of the bank. As a result, the entries are opposite to the entries in the customer's cash book.
- The debit column of a bank statement contains payments <u>out</u> of the bank. The credit column of a bank statement contains payments <u>into</u> the bank.
- A credit balance on the bank statement indicates cash in the bank. A debit balance on the bank statement indicates an overdrawn balance.

Illustration

How to update a cashbook and prepare a bank reconciliation

Ling Yeung has recently received her bank statement dated 17 March 2008 and asks you to prepare a bank reconciliation statement at that date.

The bank statement and an extract from her cash book are shown below:

Case study

Ling Yeung

Ling Yeung owns a small shop selling ladies clothes, shoes and accessories in Ealing, West London. She designs and makes some items herself, but most of her stock comes from other suppliers.

Bank Statement for Ling Yeung dated 17 March 2008

Date	Details	Dr (£)	Cr (£)	Balance (£)
7 March	Balance brought forward			1,812 Cr
7 March	Cheque 488246	100		1,712 Cr
10 March	Credit		1,615	3,327 Cr
10 March	Direct debit – property rates	168		3,159 Cr
10 March	Credit		2,607	5,766 Cr
12 March	Cheque 488245	42		5,724 Cr
12 March	Cheque 488247	117		5,607 Cr
13 March	Standing order – JK Finance	210		5,397 Cr
13 March	Credit transfer – XY Clothing		446	5,843 Cr
13 March	Cheque 488249	635		5,208 Cr
17 March	Bank charges	26		5,182 Cr
17 March	Cheque 488251	963		4,219 Cr

Ling Yeung. Cash book extract

Dr						Cr
Date	Details	£	Date	Details		£
7 March	Balance b/d	1,812	7 March	488245 P Davies		42
7 March	B West & Co	1,615	7 March	488246 Cash		100
10 March	Ford Clothing	2,607	10 March	488247 S Keene		117

17 March	Wye Leisurewear	3,260	10 March	488248 Foley & Co	1,063
			10 March	488249 HK Clothing	635
			11 March	488250 Sawyer Ltd	390
			12 March	488251 D Alsop	963
			12 March	488252 Lee Motors	112

Required

Update the cash book at 17 March 2008 and prepare a bank reconciliation statement at that date.

Approach

1 Tick all amounts that appear on both the bank statement and in the cash book.

2 Enter all items that are unticked on the bank statement into the cash book.

3 Close off the cash book and carry down the balance.

4 Start the bank reconciliation statement by entering the closing balance from the cash book.

5 Add all unpresented cheques (unticked items from the credit side of the cash book).

6 Deduct all outstanding lodgements (unticked items from the debit side of the cash book).

7 The balance on the bank reconciliation statement should now agree with the balance in the cash book.

Solution

Ling Yeung. Updated cash book					
Dr					**Cr**
Date	Details	£	Date	Details	£
7 March	Balance b/d	1,812	7 March	488245 P Davies	42
7 March	B West & Co	1,615	7 March	488246 Cash	100
10 March	Ford Clothing	2,607	10 March	488247 S Keene	117
17 March	Wye Leisurewear	3,260	10 March	488248 Foley & Co	1,063
13 March	Credit transfer XY Clothing	446	10 March	488249 HK Clothing	635
			11 March	488250 Sawyer Ltd	390
			12 March	488251 D Alsop	963
			12 March	488252 Lee Motors	112
			10 March	Direct debit propery rates	168
			13 March	Standard order JK Finance	210
			17 March	Bank charges	26
			17 March	Balance c/d	5,914
		9,740			9,740
18 March	Balance b/d	5,914			

Ling Yeung. Bank reconciliation statement at 17 March 2008			
		£	£
Balance per cash book		5,914	
Add: Unpresented cheques	488248	1,063	
	488250	390	
	488252	112	1,565
		7,479	
Deduct: Outstanding lodgements	Wye Leisurewear		3,260
Balance per bank statement			4,219

What is the importance of the bank reconciliation statement?

- It enables any errors in the cash book to be corrected.
- It enables any errors on the bank statement to be investigated and notified to the bank for correction.
- It enables any missing entries in the cash book to be accounted for.
- It acts as a deterrent to fraud because the bank statement is an independent accounting record, prepared by the bank, providing the means to verify entries in the cash book.
- It enables any out-of-date cheques to be identified (over six months old) and cancelled in the cash book.

Activity

Explain the difference between a direct debit and a standing order.

🔦✅ Learning outcomes

As a result of studying this topic, you should now be able to:

- state the purpose and importance of the bank reconciliation
- update the cash book by reference to the bank statement
- prepare a bank reconciliation statement.

 Examination-style questions

✅ **1**   Explain the meaning of the following terms relating to bank reconciliations.
  (i)   Unpresented cheque.
  (ii) Outstanding lodgement.

2   Prepare a bank reconciliation statement at 31 May 2008 from the following information, clearly identifying the balance as per the bank statement at 31 May 2008.

	£
Balance as per the cash book at 31 May 2008.	3,427
Direct debit payment 27 May 2008 not yet entered in the cash book.	50
Bank interest received 31 May 2008 not yet entered in the cash book.	1,293
Cheque drawn on 20 May 2008 and subsequently cancelled, but no cancellation had been processed through the cash book.	112
Unpresented cheques at 31 May 2008.	1,864
Outstanding lodgements at 31 May 2008.	206

3   Explain the benefits of using each of the following methods of verifying records and give examples of errors that will be revealed in each case.

(a)   Bank reconciliation statement.

(b)   Trial balance.

4   ACCI June 2004

James Baker has received a bank statement for his business and is preparing a bank reconciliation statement.

(a)   Why are bank reconciliation statements prepared?

(b)   The bank statement includes the following entries.

Explain the meaning of each of them. Identify the ledger entries James Baker will have to make.

(i)   Standing order paid to Perfect Insurance Co £200.

(ii) Credit transfer from The Magnificent Garden Centre £700.47.

(iii) Bank charges £43.27.

5   ACCI January 2006

The cash book of Western Products at 31 May 2007 shows a debit balance of £3426.67. The balance shown on the bank statement at 31 May 2007 did not agree with the cash book.

On investigation, the following was discovered:

(i)   A cheque paid for fuel on 27 May 2007 for £64.14 had been entered in the cash book, but had not yet been presented to the bank.

(ii) Cheques received from customers totalling £1325.50 had been entered in the cash book and paid into the bank on 31 May 2007. These cheques were not shown on the bank statement.

(iii) A cheque paid for advertising for £132.90 had been entered in the cash book as £123.90.

(iv) The bank had paid a direct debit for subscriptions of £55.00 on 19 May 2007, but no entry had been made in the cash book.

(v)   On 31 May, the bank had debited the account with bank charges of £115.00 and credited the account with bank interest received of £34.50. Neither of these amounts had been entered in the cash book.

(a)   Make the necessary entries in the cash book of Western Products and show the updated balance.

(b)   repare a bank reconciliation statement that clearly shows the balance on the bank statement at 31 May 2007.

(c)   Write a memorandum to the manager of Western Products explaining why it is important to prepare a bank reconciliation statement.

Cash Book

Dr								Cr
Date	Details	£	p	Date	Details	£	p
31 May	Balance b/d	3426	67				

3 Sales and purchase ledger control accounts

In this topic you will learn:

- the role, presentation and limitations of control accounts

- how to produce a sales ledger control account and a purchase ledger control account.

Sales and purchases ledger control accounts – structure

A control account is a 'master' total account and its purpose is to verify the accuracy of entries made in the subsidiary ledgers.

Remember, control accounts do NOT form part of the double entry system – they are effectively memorandum accounts.

When individual postings are made to the suppliers' accounts in the purchase ledger and the customers' accounts in the sales ledger, the totals of these postings may be transferred to the purchase ledger control account and sales ledger control account respectively.

In this way, the balance on the two control accounts should agree with the totals of the individual balances in the respective ledgers.

The structure of a typical **sales ledger control account** is as follows:

Dr				Date	Details	Cr
Date	Details		£	Date	Details	£
1 Nov	Balance b/d		80,000	30 Nov	Bank	93,000
30 Nov	Sales day book		102,000	30 Nov	Discounts allowed	2,000
30 Nov	Returned cheques		500	30 Nov	Sales returns day book	1,000
				30 Nov	Contras	1,500
				30 Nov	Bad debts written off	1,000
				30 Nov	Balance c/d	84,000
			182,500			182,500
1 Dec	Balance b/d		84,000			

Figure 3.3 *Sales ledger control account*

Guidance notes

1 **Balance b/d.** The total of all individual customer account balances at 1 November.

2 **Sales day book.** The total column in the sales day book.

3 **Returned cheques.** The total of all customer returned cheques in the period.

4 **Bank.** The total of all customer cheques and cash received in respect of credit sales only, from the cash book.

5 **Discounts allowed.** The total of the discounts allowed column from the debit side of the cash book.

6 **Sales returns day book.** The total column in the sales returns day book.

7 **Contras.** The total of all amounts set off against the purchases ledger accounts.

8 **Bad debts written off.** The total of all customer accounts that have been written off as bad debts in the period.

9 **Balance c/d.** The total of all individual customer account balances at 30 November.

Note

If any customer accounts have a credit balance rather than a debit balance, the total of these credit balances will be shown separately in the control account.

The structure of a typical purchases ledger control account is as follows:

Dr						Cr
Date	Details	£	Date	Details		£
30 Nov	Bank	66,000	1 Nov	Balance b/d		56,000
30 Nov	Discounts received	1,700	30 Nov	Purchases day book		72,000
30 Nov	Purchases returns day book	2,000	30 Nov	Cancelled cheques		1,200
30 Nov	Contras	1,500				
30 Nov	Balance c/d	58,000				
		129,200				129,200
			1 Dec	Balance b/d		58,000

Figure 3.4 *Purchases ledger control account*

Guidance notes

1 **Balance b/d.** The total of all individual supplier account balances at 1 November.

2 **Purchases day book.** The total column in the purchases day book.

3 **Cancelled cheques.** The total of all cheques drawn in favour of suppliers, but cancelled in the period.

4 **Bank.** The total of all supplier cheques and cash paid in respect of credit purchases only, from the cash book.

5 **Discounts received.** The total of the discounts received column from the credit side of the cash book.

6 **Purchases returns day book.** The total column in the purchases returns day book.

7 **Contras.** The total of all amounts set off against sales ledger accounts.

8 **Balance c/d.** The total of all individual supplier account balances at 30 November.

Note

If any supplier accounts have a debit balance rather than a credit balance, the total of these debit balances will be shown separately in the control account.

Key terms

Cancelled cheque: a cheque drawn by the business and subsequently cancelled before payment.

Contra entry: a cancellation of a debit balance with a credit balance in different books of account.

Returned cheque: a cheque that has been paid into the bank, but not honoured by the drawer's bank (usually because of lack of funds)

Activity

Explain the meaning of a contra in a purchase or sales ledger control account

Activity

Prepare a sales ledger control account for the month of April 2008 using the following information. The balance on the account should be entered as the closing balance at 30 April 2008.

	£
Sales ledger balances (debit) at 1 April 2008	66,480
Total of sales day book for April 2008	38,740
Total of sales returns day book for April 2008	614
Cash received from credit customers	44,594
Cash discounts allowed	379
Bad debts written off	125

Writing off bad debts in the sales ledger

There will be occasions when debtors are unable to pay what is owing to the business. Perhaps the customer disputes the amount owing or perhaps they have become bankrupt. These debts are then written off the customers' accounts in the sales ledger.

The process of writing off a bad debt in the sales ledger involves crediting the individual customer's account with the amount of the debt being written off.

Debit   Bad debts written off

Credit   Customer's account (in the sales ledger)

As we have seen, the control accounts do not form part of the double entry system, so in order to maintain the correct balance in the control account, the amount must also be posted to the credit of that account.

Illustration

How to prepare a purchase ledger control account

The following figures have been drawn from the books for the month ended 31 March 2001.

	£
Balances at 1 March 2001	
Credit balances	23,437
Debit balances	465
Balances at 31 March 2001	
Purchases on credit for the month	245,897
Returns to suppliers of credit purchases	4,679
Cash purchases	25,679
Purchase ledger balances set off against sales ledger	475
Cheques paid to suppliers	236,498
Discounts received	3,674
Cheque refunds from credit suppliers	450
Debit balance on the purchase ledger	749
Credit balances on the purchase ledger	?

Approach

In order to prepare the purchase ledger control account, the accountant must decide which, if any, of the items in this list do not belong in the purchase ledger control account.

The opening balance is known, but each other item should be taken in turn and a decision made as to whether it increases the balance owing or reduces it.

The final purchase ledger control account will be as follows, with the balancing figure representing the closing balances at 31 March. These could then be checked against the total of the list of balances extracted from the purchase ledger.

Dr			Purchases ledger control account				Cr
Date	Details	£	Date	Details	£		
1 March	Balances b/d	465	1 March	Balances b/d	23,437		
31 March	Returns outwards	4,679	31 March	Credit purchases	245,897		
31 March	Sales ledger contra	475	31 March	Bank	450		
31 March	Bank	236,498	31 March	Balances c/d	749		
31 March	Discounts received	3,674					
31 March	Balances c/d	24,742					
		270,533			270,533		
1 April	Balances b/d	749	1 April	Balances b/d	24,742		

Activity

The sales ledger control account for the month ended 31 October 2008 did not agree with the sales ledger balances list total.

The following errors have been discovered:

1 The sales day book was undercast by £540.

2 The returns inwards day book includes £100 that is actually for returns outwards.

3 A discount allowed of £37 has been omitted from the books completely.

4 A cheque received from J C Cross Garages for £1,479 was entered in the account of A B Cross Ltd in error.

5 The opening balance brought down should have been £25,080.

Enter the necessary corrections in the control account below and balance the account.

Dr			Sales ledger control account		Cr
Date	Details	£	Date	Details	£
31 Oct	Balance b/d	25,800			

Benefits of control accounts

Accuracy

A balanced control account verifies the arithmetical accuracy of the subsidiary ledger.

Prevention of fraud

Control accounts should be maintained by a supervisor or member of staff other than the ledger clerk with responsibility for a particular ledger. As such, this segregation of duties acts as a deterrent to fraud and makes the discovery of fraud much easier.

Management information

Management are able to view a total amount owing from customers or owing to suppliers at any time, without totalling all of the individual accounts.

Preparation of financial accounts

Having a control account balance enables interim or final accounts to be drawn up more quickly.

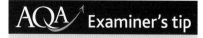

Limitations of control accounts

Individual account balances

A balanced control account verifies the **arithmetical** accuracy of the ledger; it does NOT prove that each individual account balance is correct. The following errors will not be identified.

- **Errors of omission.** Where a transaction has been completely omitted from the records.
- **Compensating error.** Where equal and opposite errors cancel each other out.
- **Error of commission.** Where an amount is posted to an incorrect account of the correct type. For example Andrew Smith account instead of Alf Smith account.
- **Error of original entry.** Where an error is made transferring an amount from the source document into the book of original entry.

Activity

Explain the benefits of using the sales ledger control account to verify records and give examples of errors that will be revealed by the control account.

Explain the main limitation of control accounts using two examples to illustrate your answer.

Link

For more information on control accounts, see A2 Module 3.

Learning outcomes

As a result of studying this topic, you should now be able to:

- state the purpose and importance of control accounts
- prepare a sales ledger control account and a purchases ledger control account
- comment on the benefits and limitations of control accounts

AQA Examination-style questions

1. Prepare a sales ledger control account for the month of April 2008 using the following information. The balance on the account should be entered as the closing balance at 30 April 2008.

	£
Sales ledger balances (debit) at 1 April 2008	66,480
Total of sales day book for April 2008	38,740
Total of sales returns day book for April 2008	614
Cash received from credit customers	44,594
Cash discounts allowed	379
Bad debts written off	125

2. From the following list of balances extracted from the books of BJ Patel on 30 November 2007, complete the sales and purchases ledger control accounts. Bring down the balance on each account.

	£
Sales on credit	26,500
Purchases on credit	19,600
Returns inwards	590
Returns outwards	450
Amounts received from customers	18,900
Amounts paid to suppliers	16,300
A debit balance set off from the sales ledger to the purchase ledger (contra)	400

Dr	Sales ledger control account				Cr
Date	Details	£	Date	Details	£
1 Nov	Balance b/d	5,476			

Dr	Purchases ledger control account				Cr
Date	Details	£	Date	Details	£
			1 Nov	Balance b/d	2,960

Explain how control accounts are used to verify the balances in the sales ledger and the purchase ledger accounts.

What is the main limitation of using a control account to verify these ledger accounts?

3   Adapted from ACC1 January 2002

House and Home have prepared the following sales ledger control account for December 2001. The following errors are then discovered

	Sales Ledger Control Account				
Dr					**Cr**
Date	**Details**	**£**	**Date**	**Details**	**£**
1 Dec	Balance b/d	32,168	31 Dec	Bank	59,861
31 Dec	Sales	45,972	31 Dec	Discount allowed	2,563
31 Dec	Returned cheque	123	31 Dec	Returns inwards	1,879
			31 Dec	Balance c/d	13,960
		78,263			78,263
1 Jan	Balance b/d	13,960			

1.   The sales day book total has been overcast by £2500.
2.   The returns inwards figure should have been £1789.
3.   There is a contra entry with the purchase ledger of £560, representing an account settled with a supplier, which has been omitted.
4.   An account for J Mason Ltd was credited with a cheque for £769; this should have been credited to J B Mason and Son.

(a)   Redraft the sales ledger control account making the entries necessary to show the correct balance to be brought down. Show your entries in the sales ledger control account below.

	Sales Ledger Control Account				
Dr					**Cr**
Date	**Details**	**£**	**Date**	**Details**	**£**
1 Dec	Balance b/d	32,168	31 Dec	Bank	59,861
31 Dec	Returned cheque	123	31 Dec	Discount allowed	2,563

(b)   What does the closing balance of a sales ledger control account represent?

(c)   How can this balance be verified?

4   ACC1 June 2006

The following information relating to the month of May 2006 has been extracted from the subsidiary books of W G Shrubb on 31 May 2006.

	£
Sales day book	43,500
Purchases day book	28,900
Returns inwards day book	625
Returns outwards day book	1,340
Discounts allowed	425
Discounts received	780
Payments received from credit customers	35,600
Payments made to credit suppliers	17,680

(a)   Prepare the sales ledger control account for the month of May 2006. Bring down the balance at 1 June 2006.

Sales Ledger Control Account

Dr					Cr
Date	Details	£	Date	Details	£

On 31 May 2006, the total of the balances extracted from the sales ledger was £17,640

(b)   Explain one benefit of using control accounts.

5   ACC1 June 2006

The following information has been extracted from the books of Delaney Paints for the month ended 30 November 2006.

	£
Sales ledger balances at 1 November 2006	23,261
Purchase ledger balances at 1 November 2006	14,908
Credit sales	14,720
Credit purchases	11,804
Returns outwards	533
Returns inwards	260
Discounts received	42
Discounts allowed	77
Payments to suppliers	9,643
Receipts from customers	15,106
Customer's cheque dishonoured	102
Contra (debit balance set off from the sales ledger to the purchase ledger)	55

Required

Prepare a sales ledger control account and a purchases ledger control account. Balance each account at 30 November 2006 and bring down the balances.

4 Final accounts

The final chapter in Unit 1 brings together all of the information that has been processed so far in the preparation of the final accounts of the business.

The final accounts comprise three main statements:

- The trading account
- The profit and loss account
- The balance sheet

Having learned how to produce the trial balance, the final step is to prepare a trading account to identify the gross profit, a profit and loss account to identify the net profit and a balance sheet to provide a statement of the business's capital, assets and liabilities at a given date.

You will also learn in this final chapter how to make simple adjustments to the final accounts in respect of:

- Closing stock
- Prepayments
- Accruals
- Bad debts
- Depreciation.

These adjustments are an introduction to an important area of study that will be further developed in Unit 2. If the final accounts were not adjusted for the items listed above, they would not represent an accurate reflection of either the profit or loss, or of the state of the business's affairs at a given date (the true and fair view).

1 The trading account, profit and loss account and balance sheet

The starting point for the preparation of the final accounts is the trial balance, listing all of the balances from the general ledger.

The final accounts of a business comprise

- Trading account
- Profit and loss account
- Balance sheet

🔆 ¹₂₃ Trading account

The trading account compares sales for the period with the **cost of sales** for the period. The difference between these two figures is the **gross profit**.

The format for a trading account is shown in Figure 4.1.

	£	£	£
Sales			XXX
Less: returns inwards			(XXX)
			XXX
Cost of sales			
Opening stock		XXX	
Purchases	XXX		
Less : returns outwards	(XXX)		
	XXX		
Add: Carriage inwards	XXX	XXX	
		XXX	
Less: Closing stock		(XXX)	XXX
Gross profit			XXX

Figure 4.1 *Trading account*

Adjustment for stock in the trading account

The value of stock that is included in the trial balance is always the opening stock. The value of closing stock will appear as additional information after the trial balance.

As we have seen, to maintain the principles of double entry, every debit must have an equal credit. In order to adhere to this rule, the value of closing stock will be as follows:

Debit: **Current assets in the balance sheet.** (Stock is an asset that the business holds at the end of the accounting period.)

Credit: **Trading account.** (Stock still held by the business reduces the cost of goods sold.)

▮ Activity

Cost of sales

Calculate the cost of sales from the following figures

Opening stock	35,000
Purchases	165,300
Returns outwards	1,800
Carriage inwards	3,400
Closing stock	32,000

In this topic you will learn:

■ the nature and purpose of the trading account

■ the nature and purpose of the profit and loss account

■ the nature and purpose of the balance sheet

■ how to prepare the trading account, profit and loss account and balance sheet from the trial balance.

▮ Background knowledge

The final accounts of a business will be prepared annually as a matter of course, but more frequently (perhaps monthly or quarterly) to inform management on how the business is performing.

AQA⁄ Examiner's tip

Returns inwards should be deducted from sales and **returns outwards** should be deducted from purchases.

▮ Key terms

Cost of sales: the total purchases plus carriage inwards adjusted for opening and closing stock on hand.

Gross profit: the difference between sales and the cost of those sales.

▮ Link

For more information on stock valuation, see Chapter 6, page 86.

■ Key terms

Net profit: the final figure on the profit and loss account when the gross profit is *greater than* the expenses that have been deducted from it.

Net loss: the final figure on the profit and loss account when the gross profit is *less than* the expenses that have been deducted from it.

■ Activity

Preparing a trading account

The following information has been extracted from the books of account of A Tate at 31 August 2008.

	£
Carriage inwards	3,763
Carriage outwards	4,078
Discounts allowed	4,221
Discounts received	**2,089**
Drawings	38,410
Purchases	212,438
Returns inwards	8,444
Returns outwards	6,204
Sales	356,270
Shop expenses	37,555
Stock at 1 September 2007	75,840
Stock at 31 August 2008	62,706

Prepare a **trading account** for the year ended 31 August 2008.

AQA Examiner's tip

■ The heading for the trading account must always be 'Trading account **for the year ended**….'

■ The heading for the profit and loss account must always be 'Profit and loss account **for the year ended**…'.

■ **Profit and loss account**

The profit and loss account commences with the gross profit brought down from the trading account, adds any other income, (for example discounts received, rents received, etc.) and deducts the expenses of running the business during the period.

If income is greater than expenditure, then a **net profit** results, but if expenditure is greater than income, then a **net loss** results.

A typical profit and loss account would appear as follows

	£	£
Gross profit		XXX
Add: Discounts received		<u>XXX</u>
		XXX
Less; expenses		
Carriage outwards	XXX	
Discounts allowed	XXX	
Motor expenses	XXX	
Office expenses	XXX	
Stationery and advertising	<u>XXX</u>	
		<u>(XXX)</u>
Net profit for the year		XXX

Figure 4.2 *Profit and loss account*

■ Link

For more information on profit and loss accounts, see Chapter 7, page 95.

Balance sheet

The balance sheet is a statement prepared at the end of an accounting period, summarising the capital account of the owner of the business and detailing the assets and liabilities representing that capital investment on a specific date.

It is important to analyse assets and liabilities under the correct sub-headings.

Fixed assets are intended to be held for more than one financial period. They are not purchased with the intention of being resold; the intention is that they should be held to generate profits for the business.

Examples of fixed assets are premises, motor vehicles, machinery, etc.

Current assets are cash or assets that will be turned into cash within the next twelve months. Current assets should be listed in reverse **order of liquidity** on the balance sheet, starting with the least liquid (stock) down to the most liquid (cash).

Examples of current assets are closing stock, debtors, prepayments, cash at bank and cash in hand.

Current liabilities are amounts owed by the business in the short term that will be paid within the next twelve months.

Examples of current liabilities are trade creditors, accruals and bank overdrafts.

Net current assets/liabilities is the difference between current assets and current liabilities.

Long-term liabilities are amounts owed by the business that are not due to be paid in the next twelve months.

Examples of long-term liabilities are bank loans and mortgages.

Capital account is the amount of the investment in the business made by the owner. The capital account on the balance sheet is represented as follows:

	£
Balance brought forward *(from the previous balance sheet)*.	XXX
Add: Capital introduced during the year.	XXX
Add: Net profit for the year *or*	XXX
Deduct: Net loss for the year	(XXX)
	XXX
Deduct: Drawings.	(XXX)
Balance carried forward *(to the next year's balance sheet)*	XXX

Figure 4.3 *Capital account*

The closing balance on the capital account will always be equal to and represented by the excess of assets over liabilities.

This conforms to the accounting equation

Assets – Liabilities = Capital

Key terms

Fixed assets: resources owned by the business intended for continuing use in running the business rather than for resale.

Current assets: resources owned by the company that are planned to be converted into cash within 12 months.

Current liabilities: monies owed by the business due for repayment within twelve months.

Net current assets/liabilities: the difference between current assets and current liabilities.

Long-term liabilities: monies owed by the business due for repayment at a time after 12 months.

Order of liquidity: the order in which current assets are able to be turned into cash.

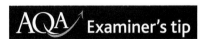

Examiner's tip

The heading for the balance sheet must always be 'Balance sheet **at** ….'

Link

For more information on balance sheets, see Chapter 7, page 88.

Activity

Balance sheet terminology

Explain the difference between:

■ Current assets and fixed assets.

■ Give one example of a current asset and one example of a fixed asset.

■ Current liabilities and long-term liabilities.

Case study

CK Traders

Chris Knight is an ex-professional footballer. When he retired from playing football two years ago, he set up his own business, CK Traders selling sportswear.

☑ Step by step guide to preparing final accounts from a trial balance

1 Identify on the trial balance items for the trading account, items for the profit and loss account and items for the balance sheet and mark these on the trial balance against each heading.

2 Draft the trading and profit and loss account headings.

3 Transfer all relevant amounts onto the trading account and calculate the gross profit.

4 Open the profit and loss account with the gross profit brought down from the trading account.

5 Transfer all relevant amounts onto the profit and loss account and calculate the net profit or loss.

6 Draft the balance sheet headings.

7 Transfer all remaining amounts onto the balance sheet.

AQA Examiner's tip

To avoid common errors, note:

■ The stock shown on the trial balance is the **opening stock**.

■ The **closing stock** is shown as a separate note after the trial balance and appears on both the trading account and the balance sheet to complete the double entry.

■ Carriage inwards appears on the trading account; carriage outwards appears on the profit and loss account. Both are expenses (debit balances).

■ Drawings appear as a deduction from the capital account. They do not appear on the profit and loss account.

■ Discounts received appear AFTER the gross profit.

■ Don't forget to show the complete heading for each of the final accounts **with no abbreviations**.

■ Show all relevant workings.

Illustration

How to prepare a trading and profit and loss account

Chris Knight's bookkeeper has extracted the following trial balance at 31 May 2008:

	Dr (£)	Cr (£)
Capital account at 1 June 2007		46,960
Carriage inwards	1,650	
Carriage outwards	1,130	
Cash at bank	2,100	
Discounts allowed	680	
Discounts received		1,450
Drawings	23,200	
Mortgage on premises (repayable 2012)		43,000
Motor expenses	3,480	
Motor vehicle at cost	18,000	
Office expenses	8,410	
Premises at cost	75,000	

	Dr	Cr
Purchases	190,340	
Returns inwards	800	
Returns outwards		400
Sales		256,200
Stationery and advertising	2,370	
Stock at 1 June 2007	32,400	
Trade creditors		32,350
Trade debtors	20,800	
Totals	**380,360**	**380,360**

Additional information
Stock at 31 May 2008 is £28,150

Required

Chris needs to prepare a trading and profit and loss account for CK
Traders for the year ended 31 May 2008 and a balance sheet at that date.

	Dr (£)	Cr (£)	Working
Capital account at 1 June 2007		46,960	Balance sheet
Carriage inwards	1,650		Trading a/c
Carriage outwards	1,130		Profit & loss a/c
Cash at bank	2,100		Balance sheet
Discounts allowed	680		Profit & loss a/c
Discounts received		1,450	Profit & loss a/c
Drawings	23,200		Balance sheet
Mortgage on premises (repayable 2012)		43,000	Balance sheet
Motor expenses	3,480		Profit & loss a/c
Motor vehicle at cost	18,000		Balance sheet
Office expenses	8,410		Profit & loss a/c
Premises at cost	75,000		Balance sheet
Purchases	190,340		Trading a/c
Returns inwards	800		Trading a/c
Returns outwards		400	Trading a/c
Sales		256,200	Trading a/c
Stationery and advertising	2,370		Profit & loss a/c

Step 1 Identify on the trial balance items for the trading account, items for the profit and loss account and items for the balance sheet and mark this on the trial balance against each heading.

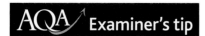
Stock at 1 June 2007	32,400		Trading a/c
Trade creditors		32,350	Balance sheet
Trade debtors	20,800		Balance sheet
Totals	**380,360**	**380,360**	

Trading a/c and balance sheet

Step 2 Draft the trading and profit and loss account headings.

Step 3 Transfer all relevant amounts onto the trading account and calculate the gross profit.

CK Traders.

Trading and profit and loss account for the year ended 31 May 2008

	£	£	£
Sales			256,200
Less: returns inwards			800
			255,400
Cost of sales			
Stock at 1 June 2007		32,400	
Purchases	190,340		
Less : returns outwards	400		
	189,940		
Carriage inwards	1,650	191,590	
		223,990	
Less: Stock at 31 May 2008		28,150	195,840
Gross profit			**59,560**
Add: Discounts received			1,450
			61,010
Less; expenses			
Carriage outwards		1,130	
Discounts allowed		680	
Motor expenses		3,480	
Office expenses		8,410	
Stationery and advertising		2,370	
			16,070
Net profit for the year			**44,940**

Step 4 Open the profit and loss account with the gross profit brought down from the trading account.

Step 5 Transfer all relevant amounts onto the profit and loss account and calculate the net profit or loss.

CK Traders.

Step 6 Draft the balance sheet headings.

Balance sheet at 31 May 2008

	£	£
Fixed assets		
Premises at cost	75,000	
Motor vehicles at cost	18,000	93,000

Current assets		
Stock on hand	28,150	
Trade debtors	20,800	
Cash at bank	2,100	
	51,050	
Current liabilities		
Trade creditors	32,350	
Net current assets		18,700
		111,700
Long-term liabilities		
Mortgage on premises (repayable 2012)		43,000
		68,700
Capital account		
Brought forward at 1 June 2008		46,960
Add: Net profit for the year		44,940
		91,900
Deduct: Drawings		23,200
		68,700

Step 7 Transfer all remaining amounts onto the balance sheet.

 *Learning outcomes*

As a result of studying this topic, you should now be able to:

- describe the structure of the trading account, the profit and loss account and the balance sheet
- prepare the headings and sub-headings in the final accounts
- prepare the final accounts from a trial balance

AQA Examination-style questions

1 Explain why each of the following may be useful to the owners of a business.
   Trading account
   Profit and loss account
   Balance sheet

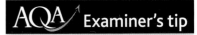 **Examiner's tip**

Clearly label the sub headings – 'Fixed assets', 'Current assets', 'Current liabilities'. 'Long-term liabilities' and 'Capital account'.

2 The following information has been extracted from the books of account of Terry Harris at 31 July 2008.

	£
Accruals	410
Bank loan (repayable January 2010)	15,700

Bank overdraft	8,296
Capital account at 1 August 2007	39,619
Carriage inwards	892
Carriage outwards	1,165
Discount allowed	817
Discount received	1,352
Drawings	32,410
Motor running expenses	8,976
Motor vehicles at cost	18,500
Prepayments	175
Purchases	72,156
Rent and rates	18,519
Returns inwards	906
Returns outwards	472
Sales	126,410
Stationery and advertising	1,220
Stock at 1 August 2007	22,640
Stock at 31 July 2008	26,450
Trade creditors	4,269
Trade debtors	3,662
Wages and salaries	14,490

Required

Prepare a trading and profit and loss account for the year ended 31 July 2008 and a balance sheet at that date.

3   Adapted from ACC1 January 2008

James Seddon runs a business selling sports equipment. The following list of balances has been extracted from the books at 31 December 2007 and from information supplied by James.

	£
Bank loan (repayable 2008)	600
Bank overdraft	7,844
Capital account at 1 December 2007	37,864
Discounts received	493
Drawings	2,200
General expenses	622
Gross profit for the month	19,320
Light & heat	815
Motor expenses	1,860
Motor vehicle at cost	12,400
Rent & rates	1,240
Stock at 31 December 2007	42,650
Trade creditors	5,692
Trade debtors	4,836
Wages & salaries	5,190

(a)   Prepare a profit and loss account for the month ending 31 December 2007.

(b)   Prepare a balance sheet as at 31 December 2007.

2 Adjustments to final accounts

In this topic you will learn:

- how to process adjustments to the final accounts in respect of:
  accruals
  prepayments
  depreciation
  bad debt write off.

☑ The final accounts we have produced so far, have all been produced directly from the closing balances from the general ledger, found in the trial balance. In reality, because the accounts are not drawn up on a cash basis, adjustments will need to be made to some of these figures to account for depreciation, bad debts, accruals and prepayments.

Depreciation

Depreciation is the apportionment of the **cost** of an asset over its **estimated useful economic life**. The value of a fixed asset falls due to age, wear and tear, obsolescence, etc. The charge for depreciation appears as an expense in the profit and loss account and represents the cost to the business of using that asset over the financial period.

Note; the only fixed asset that does not depreciate is land since this has an infinite life.

There are a number of different methods of calculating depreciation, but the only one studied in this unit is the straight-line method.

Straight-line depreciation involves spreading the **net cost** of the asset over its estimated useful economic life.

$$\text{Net cost} = \frac{\text{Cost} - \text{estimated residual value}}{\text{Estimated useful economic life}}$$

Illustration

How to calculate annual charge for depreciation

Mohammed purchases new machinery for £28,000 and estimates that its useful life will be 5 years. Mohammed estimates that the machinery will be worth £3,000 at the end of five years. Calculate the annual charge for depreciation to appear in Mohammed's final accounts for the year.

Initial cost	£28,000
Estimated residual value	£ 3,000
Net cost	£25,000

The net cost of £25,000 will be spread over the useful economic life of 5 years.

Working: £25,000/5 years = £5,000 per annum.

Key terms

Cost: the price paid for the asset.

Estimated useful economic life: the estimated time that the business will continue to use the asset.

Net cost: initial cost of the asset less the estimated residual value at the end of the asset's useful economic life.

Estimated residual value: the estimated value of the asset at the end of its useful life.

Accounting entries for depreciation

As with all accounting entries, we must maintain the principles of double entry. As already stated, the value of assets fall as they depreciate and to take account of this reduction in value, an account is opened for provision for depreciation account, representing the accumulated depreciation of the asset. At the end of the financial year, the provision for depreciation account is credited with the charge for depreciation for the year.

    Dr   Depreciation (profit and loss account)
    Cr   Provision for depreciation account

Link

For more information on depreciation, see Chapter 7, page 101.

When completing the final accounts, the credit balance on the provision for depreciation account is deducted from the fixed asset at cost account to leave a net book value of the asset appearing on the balance sheet (see the illustration below).

*Note: Candidates will **not** be required to make ledger account entries for depreciation.*

Illustration

A trial balance and balance sheet

Trial balance (extract)

	Dr (£)	Cr (£)
Motor vehicle cost	18,000	
Motor vehicle provision for depreciation		6,000

Balance sheet (extract)

Fixed assets	(£)	(£)
Motor vehicle cost	18,000	
Motor vehicle provision for depreciation	6,000	12,000

AQA Examiner's tip

An examination question may state that depreciation is to be calculated at 10% per annum using the straight-line method.

In these circumstances, the depreciation charge for the year will be 10% of the cost of the asset.

Activity

Depreciation

Martin purchase new machinery at a cost of £12,400. He estimates that the useful life of the machinery will be five years and that at the end of five years it will have a net realisable value of £400.

1 Calculate the annual depreciation charge using the straight-line method of depreciation.

2 Calculate the book value of the machinery at the end of three years.

Link

For more information on bad debts, see Chapter 7, page 88.

Bad debt write off

As we have seen in the section on control accounts, there will be occasions when debtors are unable to pay what is owing to the business. Perhaps the customer disputes the amount owing or perhaps they have become bankrupt. These debts are then written off the customers' accounts in the sales ledger. This write off is an expense to the business and must therefore be charged in the profit and loss account, so that the final accounts reflect the correct position.

If we fail to write off a debt that is not going to be recovered, the effect will be twofold.

1 The profit will be overstated by the amount of the bad debt, and

2 The balance sheet will not reflect the correct position – debtors will be overstated by the amount of the bad debt.

AQA Examiner's tip

Bad debts come up in an examination question.

If you are provided with a trial balance that includes a debit balance for bad debts, this will simply be recorded in the profit and loss account as an expense.

Illustration

How to include an expense in the profit and loss account

Bob has produced a trial balance that includes the following figure:

	Dr (£)	Cr (£)
Bad debts written off	516	

The fact that this amount is already in the trial balance shows that the debt has already been written off and you are given no instruction as regards writing off a bad debt.

Action: Include the £516 as an expense in the profit and loss account. No further action is required.

You may be given an instruction to write off a particular bad debt. In these circumstances, you will record the bad debt in the profit and loss account as an expense and also reduce debtors by the same amount. In other words:

Debit   Bad debts written off (profit and loss account)

Credit   Debtors (balance sheet)

Illustration

How to increase bad debts written off and reduce debtors

Chris has produced a trial balance that includes the following figures:

	Dr (£)	Cr (£)
Bad debts written off	120	
Debtors	12,500	

You are told that a debt outstanding from David of £350 is outstanding, but will not be paid because David is now bankrupt. Write off the debt outstanding from David.

You are given a clear instruction to write off the bad debt.

Action: Increase bad debts written off by £350 and reduce debtors by £350. The amounts to appear in the final accounts will be as follows:

Bad debts written off £470 (£120 + £350)

Debtors £12,150 (£12,500 – £350)

Accrual of expenses

An accrual is a liability for services that have already been used, but that have not yet been invoiced to the business.

To account for accruals in the final accounts

- Increase the expense charge from the trial balance by the amount of the accrual.
- Include the amount of the accrual in the balance sheet as a current liability.

Activity

Detail the bookkeeping entries required to write off a bad debt and state the effect that writing off a bad debt will have on the profit for the year.

■ **Illustration**

How to accrual expenses

Anna has produced a trial balance at 30 May 2008 that includes the following figure:

	Dr (£)	Cr (£)
Electricity	1,430	

You are told that Anna has used £150 electricity that has not yet been billed. Provide an accrual for this amount.

Action: Increase electricity by £150, the amount that has been used but not yet billed and include the accrual on the balance sheet as a current liability

In this way, the charge for electricity in the profit and loss account will be £1,580, representing the amount of electricity actually used.

To account for accruals

Using the above illustration, the entry to account for the accrual is as follows:

Debit	Electricity	£150
Credit	Accruals	£150

Since the accrual of £150 is to be carried forward into the next accounting period, the ledger account will appear as follows:

Dr			Electricity			Cr
Date	**Details**	**£**	**Date**	**Details**		**£**
31 May	Balance (trial balance)	1,430	31 May	Profit and loss account		1,580
31 May	Balance c/d	150				
		1,580				1,580
			1 June	Balance b/d		150

■ **Activity**

Accruals

Marion has prepared the trial balance at 30 June 2008, but has now been told that an accrual is required for £350 in respect of telephone charges. Enter the accrual in the telephone charges account below and close off the account by transferring the correct amount to the profit and loss account.

Dr			Telephone charges			Cr
Date	**Details**	**£**	**Date**	**Details**		**£**
30 June	Balance b/d	3,495				

Prepayment of expenses

A prepayment arises when an expense is paid in advance and all or part of the payment relates to the next accounting period.

To account for prepayments in the final accounts.

▓ Reduce the expense charge from the trial balance by the amount of the prepayment.

▓ Include the amount of the prepayment in the balance sheet as a current asset.

▓ Illustration

How to calculate prepayment

Adit has produced a trial balance that includes the following figure:

	Dr (£)	Cr (£)
Rates	2,400	

You are told that Adit paid £2,400 for rates in April 2007 for the twelve months ending 31 March 2008. Adit is now preparing his final accounts for the year ending 31 December 2007. Calculate the amount of the prepayment for rates and provide for this in the final accounts.

Action: The amount of rates for the current accounting period is £2,400/12 months × 9 months (the nine months from April 2007 to December 2007). Therefore three months (January 2008 to March 2008) are paid in advance. The amount of the prepayment is £2,400 / 12 months × 3 months = £600.

To process the prepayment, decrease rates by £600 and include the prepayment of £600 on the balance sheet as a current asset.

In this way, the charge for rates in the profit and loss account will be £1,800 representing the nine-months charge relating to the current financial year.

To account for prepayments

Using the above illustration, the entry to account for the prepayment is as follows:

Debit	Prepayments	£600
Credit	Rates	£600

Since the prepayment of £600 is to be carried forward into the next accounting period, the ledger account will appear as follows:

Dr			Rates			Cr
Date	**Details**	**£**	**Date**	**Details**		**£**
30 April	Bank	2,400	31 Dec	Profit and loss account		1,800
			31 Dec	Balance c/d		600
		2,400				2,400
1 Jan	Balance b/d	600				

▓ Link

For more information on adjustments, see Chapter 7, page 90.

Activity

Accruals and prepayments

Tom is preparing his accounts for the year ended 30 September 2008. On 1 January 2008, he made the following payments

	£
Rent (£300 per month)	2,400
Rates (£250 per quarter)	1,000

Calculate

- The charge to appear in the profit and loss account for rent and rates.
- The amounts to appear on the balance sheet for accruals and prepayments.

Case study

Northern Sports

Northern Sports is a wholesale business supplying sportswear based in Leicester. The business was started five years ago by Cheryl McGowan and has gone from strength to strength as personal fitness has become more important to people's lifestyles.

Illustration

How to deal with adjustments

Cheryl's bookkeeper has extracted the following trial balance at 30 June 2008 and supplied the additional information as detailed.

	Dr (£)	Cr (£)
Bank overdraft		15,443
Capital account at 1 July 2007		76,961
Carriage inwards	2,701	
Carriage outwards	2,465	
Discounts allowed	1,190	
Discounts received		2,731
Drawings	26,475	
Heating and lighting	3,928	
Mortgage on premises (repayable 2015)		86,000
Motor expenses	8,435	
Motor vehicles at cost	36,400	
Office expenses	2,660	
Premises at cost	138,000	

Property repairs	2,085	
Provision for depreciation motor vehicles		7,280
Provision for depreciation shop fittings		5,680
Purchases	214,560	
Returns inwards	3,771	
Returns outwards		1,638
Sales		412,804
Shop fittings at cost	28,400	
Stock at 1 July 2007	83,480	
Trade creditors		16,196
Trade debtors	33,772	
Wages and salaries	36,411	
Totals	**624,733**	**624,733**

Additional information

1 Stock at 30 June 2008 was valued at £78,250.

2 Motor expenses were prepaid by £85.

3 Accrue £132 in respect of heating and lighting.

4 Depreciate Motor vehicles at 25% using the straight-line method of depreciation.

5 Depreciate shop fittings at 10% per annum using the straight-line method of depreciation.

6 Write off bad debts of £382

Approach

Step 1 Having identified where all of the trial balance items are to be allocated in the final accounts, deal with each of the adjustments in turn.

▪ The stock at 30 June 2008 is a current asset on the balance sheet and will reduce the cost of sales on the trading account.

▪ Dr Stock (balance sheet current assets)

▪ Cr Stock (trading account)

Step 2 The prepayment of £85 for motor expenses relates to the next accounting period. It will therefore reduce the charge for motor expenses this year and be a current asset on the balance sheet.

▪ Dr Prepayments (balance sheet current assets)

▪ Cr Motor expenses (profit and loss account)

Step 3 The accrual of £132 for heating and lighting has not yet been invoiced to the business, but has been used and will therefore increase the charge for heating and lighting in the current accounting period and the amount owing will be a current liability on the balance sheet.

▪ Dr Heating and lighting (profit and loss account)

▪ Cr Accruals (balance sheet current liabilities)

Step 4 The annual depreciation charge for motor vehicles is to be calculated at 25% based on the cost of the assets.

£36,400 × 25% = £9,100. The charge for the year is an expense in the profit and loss account and will increase the provision for depreciation on the balance sheet.

▦ Dr Depreciation (profit and loss account)

▦ Cr Provision for depreciation motor vehicles (balance sheet)

Step 5 The annual depreciation charge for shop fittings is to be calculated at 10% based on the cost of the assets.

£28,400 × 10% = £2,840. The charge for the year is an expense in the profit and loss account and will increase the provision for depreciation on the balance sheet.

▦ Dr Depreciation (profit and loss account)

▦ Cr Provision for depreciation shop fittings (balance sheet)

Step 6 Writing off the bad debts of £382 is an expense in the profit and loss account and will reduce debtors on the balance sheet.

▦ Dr Bad debts (profit and loss account)

▦ Cr Debtors (balance sheet current assets)

Working sheet

	Dr (£)	Cr (£)	Adjust Dr (£)	Adjust Cr (£)	
Bank overdraft		15,443			Balance sheet
Capital account at 1 July 2007		76,961			Balance sheet
Carriage inwards	2,701				Trading account
Carriage outwards	2,465				Profit and loss a/c
Discounts allowed	1,190				Profit and loss a/c
Discounts received		2,731			Profit and loss a/c
Drawings	26,475				Balance sheet
Heating and lighting	3,928		132		Profit and loss a/c
Mortgage on premises (repayable 2015)		86,000			Balance sheet
Motor expenses	8,435			85	Profit and loss a/c
Motor vehicles at cost	36,400				Balance sheet
Office expenses	2,660				Profit and loss a/c
Premises at cost	138,000				Balance sheet
Property repairs	2,085				Profit and loss a/c
Provision for depreciation motor vehicles		7,280		9,100	Balance sheet
Provision for depreciation shop fittings		5,680		2,840	Balance sheet
Purchases	214,560				Trading account
Returns inwards	3,771				Trading account
Returns outwards		1,638			Trading account
Sales		412,804			Trading account

Shop fittings at cost	28,400				Balance sheet
Stock at 1 July 2007	83,480				Trading account
Trade creditors		16,196			Balance sheet
Trade debtors	33,772			382	Balance sheet
Wages and salaries	36,411				Profit and loss a/c
Stock at 30 June 2008 (trading account)				78,250	Trading account
Stock at 30 June 2008 (balance sheet)			78,250		Balance sheet
Prepayments			85		Balance sheet
Accruals				132	Balance sheet
Depreciation			9,100		
			2,840		Profit and loss a/c
Bad debts			382		Profit and loss a/c
Totals	624,733	624,733	90,789	90,789	

Solution

Northern Sports

Trading and profit and loss account for the year ended 30 June 2008

	£	£	£
Sales			412,804
Less: returns inwards			3,771
			409,033
Cost of sales			
Stock at I July 2007		83,480	
Purchases	214,560		
Less : returns outwards	1,638		
	212,922		
Carriage inwards	2,701	215,623	
		299,103	
Less: Stock at 30 June 2008		78,250	220,853
Gross profit			188,180
Add: Discounts received			2,731
			190,911
Less; expenses			
Bad debts		382	
Carriage outwards		2,465	
Depreciation		11,940	
Discounts allowed		1,190	
Heating and lighting		4,060	
Motor expenses		8,350	
Office expenses		2,660	
Property repairs		2,085	
Wages and salaries		36,411	
			69,543
Net profit for the year			121,368

Northern Sports

Balance sheet at 30 June 2008

	£	£
FIXED ASSETS		
Premises at cost		138,000
Motor vehicles at cost	36,400	
Less: provision for depreciation	16,380	20,020
Shop fittings at cost	28,400	
Less: provision for depreciation	8,520	19,880
		177,900
CURRENT ASSETS		
Stock	78,250	
Trade debtors	33,390	
Prepayments	85	
	111,725	
CURRENT LIABILITIES		
Trade creditors	16,196	
Accruals	132	
Bank overdraft	15,443	
	31,771	
Net current assets		79,954
		257,854
LONG-TERM LIABILITIES		
Mortgage on premises (repayable 2015)		86,000
		171,854
CAPITAL ACCOUNT		
Brought forward		76,961
Add: Net profit for the year		121,368
		198,329
Deduct: Drawings		26,475
		171,854

☑💡 *Learning outcomes*

As a result of studying this topic, you should now be able to:

- adjust final accounts to take account of closing stock, accruals, prepayments, depreciation and bad debts written off
- process adjustments to an incorrect balance sheet

Examination-style questions

☑ 1 (a) Explain the reasons for depreciating fixed assets.

(b) Explain the difference between the charge for depreciation in the profit and loss account and the provision for depreciation that appears in the balance sheet.

2 Keelby Motors is a motor repair business. Prior to the preparation of final accounts for the year ended 31 July 2008, they consider that the debts outstanding on the following two customer accounts should be written off.

Dr			B W Motors			Cr
Date	Details	£	Date	Details		£
28 Feb	Sales day book	115				
		___				___
		___				___

Dr			Cross Garage			Cr
Date	Details	£	Date	Details		£
31 Jan	Sales day book	58				
28 Feb	Sales day book	87				
		___				___
		___				___

(a) Complete the bookkeeping entries required to write off the bad debts in the above customer accounts.

(b) The current balance on the sales ledger control account is £26,706. Show any necessary adjustments to this account.

(c) Draw up the bad debts account at 31 July 2008.

3 Alan Richmond owns a picture-framing business. Write a memorandum to Alan Richmond advising him in which section of the balance sheet the following items should appear, giving detailed reasons for your choice.

(a) Cost of new machinery purchased.

(b) Drawings for the year.

(c) Stock of frames for resale.

(d) Prepayment of two months rates.

(e) Net profit for the year.

4 Adapted from ACC3 January 2007

Samina Hussein is a trader. She provides the following information for the year ended 31 December 2006.

	£
Gross profit	110,707
Wages	62,400
Rent and rates	8,430
General expenses	9,477

Discounts received	388
Discounts allowed	307
Equipment at cost at 31 December 2006	12,000
Provision for depreciation on equipment at 1 January 2006	4,800

Additional information not yet recorded in the accounts at 31 December 2006

1   Rates paid in advance amounted to £120.

2   Rent owing amounted to £600.

3   Samina provides for depreciation on equipment at 10% using the straight-line method.

Prepare a profit and loss account for the year ended 31 December 2006.

5   Adapted from ACC3 June 2005

The following balances have been extracted from the books of Rachel Sorcim at 31 March 2005.

	Debit £	Credit £
Capital		86,048
Sales		81,643
Purchases	38,642	
Office wages	21,347	
Rent, rates and insurance	4,990	
General expenses	16,281	
Bad debts written off	49	
Premises at cost	70,000	
Equipment at cost	28,000	
Provision for depreciation on premises at 1 April 2004		16,800
Provision for depreciation on equipment at 1 April 2004		16,530
Debtors and creditors	1,260	981
Stock at 1 April 2004	1,487	
Drawings	16,500	

Additional information at 31 March 2005 not yet included by Rachel

1   Closing stock £1638.

2   Wages accrued £412.

3   Insurance paid in advance £146.

4   Rachel provides for depreciation of fixed assets as follows:

      ■ premises at 2% per annum on cost using the straight-line method;

      ■ equipment at 20% per annum on cost using the straight-line method.

(a)   Prepare a trading and profit and loss account for the year ended 31 March 2005.

(b)   Prepare an extract from the balance sheet as at 31 March 2005 showing the capital section only.

6   Adapted from ACC3 June 2004

The following trial balance has been extracted from the books of account of Siobhan Huggett on 30 April 2004.

	Debit £	Credit £
Vehicles at cost	160,000	
Equipment at cost	85,000	
Provision for depreciation on vehicles at 1 May 2003		80,400
Provision for depreciation on equipment at 1 May 2003		21,000
Stock at 1 May 2003	7,800	
Debtors and creditors	9,000	7,460
Purchases and sales	149,400	293,100
Wages and general expenses	116,200	
Business rates	13,510	
Bad debts written off	750	
Bank balance		11,450
Drawings	18,500	
Capital		146,750
TOTALS	560,160	560,160

Additional information and instructions

1 At 30 April 2004, stock was valued at £8700.
2 On 17 January 2004, Siobhan purchased equipment for £23 000. This amount is included in the purchases figure on the trial balance.
3 Wages and general expenses accrued and due at 30 April 2004 amounted to £1600.
4 Business rates paid in advance on 30 April 2004 amounted to £180.
5 Depreciation is to be provided on the value of fixed assets held at the financial year end as follows:

equipment 10% straight-line method;
vehicles 20% straight-line method.

Prepare a trading and profit and loss account for the year ended 30 April 2004.

7 Brian Jarvis has prepared the following balance sheet at the end of the accounting year. It contains errors

Balance sheet for the year ended 31 December 2005

	£	£
FIXED ASSETS		90,000
CURRENT ASSETS		
Stock	8,000	
Debtors	13,000	
Cash at bank	7,000	
	28,000	
CURRENT LIABILITIES		
Creditors	8,000	
		36,000
		54,000

CAPITAL

Opening balance	82,000
Net profit for the year	50,000
	32,000
Drawings	22,000
	54,000

Additional information

1   Fixtures and fittings costing £3,000 had been recorded as purchases and charged to the trading account for the year.

2   Brian had taken £1,000 cash from the bank account for his own use. This had not been recorded in the accounts.

3   Brian found a cheque for £2,500 received from a customer during December, which had been mislaid and had not been recorded.

Required

Redraft the balance sheet, correcting any errors.

Financial and management accounting

Chapters in this unit

Introduction to Unit 2

As you start this new unit you should feel you have developed skills in preparing double entry accounting records for a sole trader. You should also feel competent in preparing trading accounts, profit and loss accounts and balance sheets. All the work you have done to date will now be valuable as you focus your attention on this new unit, in which you are going to develop much more skill in preparing final accounts and balance sheets, and broaden your understanding of accounting principles and of the main types of business ownership.

In **Chapter 5** you are going to look at the three main types of business organisation: sole traders, partnership and limited liability companies. You are going to find out why each of these types would be appropriate for particular circumstances.

In **Chapter 6** you are going to develop an understanding of the fundamental rules that all accountants use when preparing accounting records. These fundamental rules are normally referred to as "accounting concepts". You will find that you have been applying many of these rules already without realising it.

Chapter 7 provides an opportunity for you to develop your skills in preparing final accounts and balance sheets. You will be able to use your knowledge of making adjustments applying these procedures to income such as rent receivable. You will learn how to ensure that a business's profit is calculated as realistically as possible by ensuring that some account is taken of the likelihood of there being bad debts. You will also extend your knowledge of depreciation. This chapter will also help you make sure you can distinguish correctly between amounts spent on everyday running costs and money spent on fixed assets, that is correctly identify revenue and capital expenditure.

In **Chapter 8** you will apply your understanding of final accounts and balance sheets to limited liability companies. As well as preparing company final accounts you will learn about much of the terminology that is commonly associated with limited companies. You will also learn some advanced techniques that are used to revalue fixed assets, issue shares to existing shareholders ('rights issues') and restructure a company's balance sheet by making what is often called a bonus issue of shares.

In **Chapter 9** you will learn how to make use of financial accounting information and how to provide the owner of a business, the manager of the business, or other interested parties, with data about how the business is performing. This important process is achieved by using accounting ratios and by interpreting the results of ratio calculations.

You will learn how to write effective reports on business performance that provide a reliable evaluation of performance and include recommendations on how to make further progress. In other words you will be helping the owner(s) of businesses to manage their business more effectively.

Chapter 10 introduces the idea of preparing information about the future of a business instead of looking back to what has already happened. The chapter is concerned with budgets. You will learn why budgets are a potentially valuable tool for business owners and managers, but also why budgets, if not used properly, can cause problems for businesses. You will also learn how to prepare a cash budget.

In the final chapter – **Chapter 11** – you will have the opportunity to consider why almost all businesses rely on computers and computer software to produce their financial records. You will learn about the overwhelming advantages of computerisation, but also consider the potential disadvantages of relying on computers and software programmes to produce accounting information.

When you are assessed on this unit you can expect to be asked to prepare the final accounts and balance sheets of sole traders as well as limited companies. Questions could range from those requiring a short response, requiring just a small section of a business's final accounts and/or balance sheet, to those requiring a much more extensive answer encompassing most if not all of these financial statements. In addition, questions requiring a computational response could require ledger accounts in which you demonstrate your understanding of a variety of topics, for example provisions for deprecation, provisions for doubtful debts, etc. You might also, of course, be asked to calculate ratios or prepare a cash budget.

Do not forget that you will also be asked to write about accounting topics as well. Expect to have to respond to questions requiring explanations of accounting concepts or techniques. There could be questions requiring a more lengthy response, perhaps a report in which you set out an evaluation or discussion about a particular topic, for example a business's performance or the arguments for and against forms of ownership or computerising accounting records.

5 Types of business organisation

Links

■ Partnerships are covered in more detail in *Accounting*, Unit 3.

■ Limited companies are covered in more detail in Chapter 7.

Key terms

Sole trader: a business owned by one individual. The individual bears sole responsibility for the business's actions.

Unlimited liability: the owner of a business is fully responsible for all the debts of the business.

This chapter compares three important types of business organisation. You will be able to gain an understanding of the broad range of factors that need to be considered before deciding which type of organisation is the most appropriate depending on circumstances. You will find that you are already very familiar with sole traders from the subject matter you have already covered. For example, from preparing double entry accounts and final accounts, you will know that a sole trader provides all the capital in this type of business, and is rewarded by having access to any profits in the form of drawings. You will also be aware that a sole trader has to take full responsibility for the business's activities. However, this chapter is likely to introduce you to partnerships and to limited companies for the first time.

Sole traders

What are the advantages of being a sole trader?

The **sole trader** is the only person responsible for the business and so decision making is potentially faster. Owners of this type of organisation often say that they enjoy the feeling of independence and being in control. Furthermore, sole-trader businesses are usually reasonably straightforward to establish because there are (normally) relatively few bureaucratic requirements. Of course, all the profits made by the business belong to the sole trader and these can be withdrawn in the form of cash drawings.

What are the disadvantages?

Sole traders have **unlimited liability** for the debts of their business, so if the business fails they could lose both the business's assets and also their private possessions.

The amount of capital that can be invested is likely to be limited to the wealth of one individual and this could restrict the size of the business.

Sole traders often find owning a business a great tie; some sole traders work long hours, have few holidays and sometimes rather poor rewards. They can sometimes feel they operate in isolation and do not have the support or access to the expertise available in other forms of ownership.

On the death of the sole trader the business would cease to operate.

Case study

Sally Amis becomes a sole trader

Sally Amis started her business in 1995 offering home owners advice on interior design. She had studied interior design at college and with limited private resources she found it relatively easy to start her business. She visited her customers' homes offering advice on soft furnishings and décor. She gained a lot of satisfaction from being in charge of her own affairs, but she worked very long hours and, without anyone else to discuss ideas with, found she did make a number of mistakes, some of them rather costly. It took a number of years to build up the business's reputation and a strong customer base, and profits were relatively low to start with.

Partnerships

What are the advantages of being in partnership?

Partners have access to more finance than a sole trader because there are more individuals who can make capital contributions.

Partnerships are quite often formed so that the particular expertise or specialised skills and knowledge of individuals can be guaranteed to be available. In addition, partners can often share the management responsibilities of a business, making the workload more manageable and making it possible to share ideas.

What are the disadvantages?

Partnerships, like sole traders, have unlimited liability for the debts of the business. Moreover, partners have to share whatever profits or losses are made by the business.

Decision making can be more difficult because it will be necessary to obtain the agreement of all the partners to important aspects of running the business. Sometimes good ideas may have to be abandoned because one or more partners will not agree to their implementation.

Partnerships can be relatively short-lived because they may close on the death or retirement of a partner.

Case study

Sally forms a partnership with Riccardo Verdi

Sally Amis's interior design business was doing quite well by 2001. Sally was aware, however, that in order to expand she would need more finance, and she was also aware that she needed to gain more expertise in order to offer advice about the latest developments in paints and emulsions. Since 1998 she had occasionally worked with a friend of hers, Riccardo Verdi, who had not only the private resources but also the expertise she needed. Early in 2002, Sally and Riccardo formed a partnership. Immediately the new firm of Amis and Verdi was able to offer a much fuller service to many more customers. Profits were higher than for Sally's business as a sole trader. However, these profits now had to be shared between Sally and Riccardo. Sally noticed that she was less likely to make mistakes simply because she could talk things through with Riccardo. As a result they were both able to offer better advice to customers. Sally and Riccardo generally got on very well together, but there were times when they found it difficult to reach agreement on some important decisions.

Activities

Consider the case of Sally Amis and Riccardo Verdi as they form their partnership.

1 Summarise in a few words two main advantages of Sally and Riccardo being a partnership.

2 Summarise in a few words two main disadvantages of Sally and Riccardo being a partnership.

Limited liability companies

What are the advantages of forming a limited liability company?

- Shareholders in a **limited liability company** enjoy the protection of **'limited liability'** which means that if the company fails they can lose the amount they have invested (or promised to invest) but no more. Unlike a sole trader or partner they do not risk losing their private possessions.
- Limited companies can raise large amounts of finance. There is the potential to have many shareholders investing in a company. Because companies have a separate legal identify to that of their owners, they can continue to operate irrespective of changes in ownership.
- There is the possibility of sharing ideas and management of the business with a wider group of individuals.

What are the disadvantages?

- Limited liability companies are subject to many legal requirements. For example, it is more difficult to form a limited company and, once established, directors are required to send a copy of the company's annual accounts to the Registrar of Companies; except in the case of the smallest companies, their accounts must be audited.
- From the point of view of those who first establish a limited company, there is the possibility that the control of the company could change over time as individual shareholders acquire or sell shares. This is because shares normally carry voting rights that can be used at shareholders' meetings, and so whoever owns more than 50% of the shares with voting rights, effectively controls the company.

Case study

Sally and Riccardo establish a limited company

Sally and Riccardo's partnership prospered. By 2006 they found that demand for their interior design advice was so great that they often had to turn customers away. They both felt that there was a real opportunity to expand their business still further, but that this would require far more capital. They were also very conscious that if things went wrong, they could lose all the money they had invested in the partnership and their private possessions as well. They decided the best way forward was to form a private limited company, Amis Verdi Ltd. Sally and Riccardo owned the majority of the shares in the company and they became the company's directors with responsibility for the day-to-day management of the business. Some of their key staff also became shareholders. All the shareholders clearly understood that the maximum they could lose was the amount they invested in the company's shares. The

Key terms

Limited liability company: a form of organisation whose owners (or members) own shares and where the owners enjoy the benefit of having limited liability for the debts of the business. Companies have a separate existence from their owners.

Limited liability: the responsibility of the owners of the business (shareholders) for the debts of the business is limited to the amount they have agreed to invest.

Background knowledge

There are two principle types of limited company. A private limited company (Ltd) must have one or more members (shareholders) but its shares are not available to the general public. A public limited company (plc) must have at least two shareholders and can offer shares to the public. A public limited company must have issued shares to the value of at least £50,000 before it can trade.

Link

Limited liability companies and the preparation of their final accounts are covered in more detail in Chapter 8. See page 110 for more background information about limited liability companies.

company's founders soon realised that they had to comply with many regulations when setting up the company. For example, the company had to be registered at Companies House and this meant sending several documents and completing complicated forms.

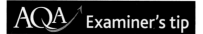

Activities

Consider the case of Sally and Riccardo as they convert their partnership into a private limited liability company.

1 Summarise in a few words two main advantages that will be enjoyed by Sally and Riccardo as the major shareholders in Amis Verdi Ltd.

2 Summarise in a few words two main disadvantages that may be arise from forming a private limited liability company.

Learning outcomes

As a result of studying this chapter, you should now be able to:

- define the terms sole trader, partnership, limited liability company, limited liability and unlimited liability
- explain the advantages and disadvantages of being a sole trader and being in a partnership
- explain the advantages and disadvantages of forming a limited liability company
- compare and evaluate the different types of ownership
- prepare a statement or report advising an individual or individuals whether or not to adopt a particular form of ownership

AQA Examiner's tip

Remember in an evaluation question like Question 3, you are expected to present a balanced argument and to come to a clear recommendation.

AQA Examiner's tip

Notice the clear focus for Question 2 (decision making). Avoid putting in points of comparison that are to do with other matters.

AQA Examination-style questions

☑ 1 Describe one advantage and one disadvantage of being:

   (i) a sole trader

   (ii) a partnership

   (iii) a limited liability company.

	Advantage	Disadvantage
Sole trader		
Partnership		
Limited liability company		

2 From the point of view of decision making, compare sole traders and partnerships as forms of business ownership.

3 A sole trader has decided to convert his business into a private limited company. Discuss the benefits and drawbacks of this decision.

6 Accounting concepts

In this chapter you will learn:

- how to explain the purpose of accounting concepts

- how to explain the rule covered by each concept and the reason for that rule

- how to apply each concept to a variety of situations, making it clear what the correct accounting treatment should be.

All the accounting procedures and techniques that you are learning as part of your A Level course follow a set of basic rules that have been carefully developed by the accountancy profession. Knowledge of these rules will enable you gain a better understanding of some new techniques and procedures that you will be learning in this and subsequent units. You will find that you have already been applying these rules without realising it, in much of the subject matter you have covered so far. For example, you will remember how, in Unit 1, you learned the technique for adjusting expenses for prepayments or amounts due when preparing a profit and loss account. This technique is based on a basic accounting rule called the 'accruals concept' that is covered in this chapter. As a second example, you will be quite used by now to recording the removal of the business's cash by the owner for private use in a separate drawings account. This transaction is recorded in this way as a result of the 'entity concept', which is also explained more fully in this chapter. Accounting concepts affect virtually every aspect of financial accounting and you will find that they are often referred to as you proceed through the remainder of this unit and through the main elements of the A2 accounting course.

Purpose of accounting concepts

What is the point of accounting concepts?

Accounting concepts are the fundamental rules that are to be followed by all those preparing accounting records. These rules ensure that everyone treats particular situations in the same way. An understanding of the concepts is vital for anyone preparing accounting records because they provide guidelines for the treatment of new or unfamiliar accounting problems. As a result, those using accounting statements can be confident in the information, because they can feel assured that the content would have been very much the same whichever accountant had prepared the statements.

You will find that many of the concepts seem like common sense. This is partly because you have unconsciously been applying them already.

Objectivity

Wherever possible, accounting information should be factual (that is objective) rather than someone's opinion (that is subjective). Accountants prefer facts, rather than opinion, because normally facts can be more easily agreed, where someone's opinion is likely to be disputed.

The **objectivity** concept is at the heart of any rules about valuing assets (see the cost concept).

Note: in some situations, of course, opinion cannot be avoided. The depreciation charge on a fixed asset depends on estimates of economic life, possible residual value, and the method of depreciation to be used.

AQA Examiner's tip

You would not be alone if you found these concepts quite difficult to grasp initially. It may help to spread out this topic over a period of time (perhaps a few days, or even a few weeks) doing a little at a time, and gradually building up an understanding.

Key terms

Objectivity: factual information is preferred because it is likely to be beyond dispute.

Cost

Assets should be valued at **cost**. This is because this is an objective valuation (see objectivity) rather than a matter of opinion.

Case study

Sally Thomas applies the cost and objectivity concepts

Sally Thomas, who owns a business called Thomas & Co, has been told that some office equipment, which originally cost £12,000 and on which depreciation of £8,000 has been charged, would now cost £14,500 to replace. Sally wonders whether the equipment's value should be adjusted to take account of the increasing cost of replacement. Sally is advised by the business's accountant to ignore the replacement value of the equipment. The accountant has said that it is uncertain just how much it would cost to replace these assets, because it would depend on many factors including which supplier was used. In other words, £14,500 as a value is a matter of opinion (subjective), whereas the original cost of £12,000 can be established by the evidence in the form of invoices for the equipment (objective). The business should continue to value the office equipment objectively using cost.

Going concern

Those preparing financial statements are to assume that the business will continue to trade for the foreseeable future (at least one year). As a result the possible resale value of assets can definitely be ignored, because the assumption is that the assets are not for sale. In other words, the **going concern** concept supports the idea of using cost as the basis of valuing assets.

Note: the going concept would have to be set aside, however, if it was known that a business, or part of a business, is likely to close in the near future.

Case study

Greg Hardy applies the going concern concept

Greg Hardy, who owns a business called Hardy Cycles, has been told that some office furniture that cost £12,000 and on which depreciation £8,000 has been written off, is likely to have a resale value of only £500. Greg wonders whether the furniture should be reduced in value in the business's books. Greg is advised by the business's accountant to ignore the possible resale value of the furniture because the business is going to continue to trade and it will make use of the office furniture for the foreseeable future.

Activity

Harry Roberts is the owner of a business that includes a motor vehicle among its fixed assets. Harry is able to supply the following information about this vehicle:

- the motor vehicle cost £25,000 when it was purchased several years ago
- a similar model would now cost £28,000 to buy
- if the vehicle was offered for sale a local dealer would be prepared to offer £21,000 for it.

Referring to as many relevant accounting concepts as possible, explain how you would value this motor vehicle in the business's books of account. Comment on whether there are any circumstances when you think it might be appropriate to use the local dealer's valuation of £21,000.

Accruals

Profits should be calculated for a period of time, ensuring that revenue for that period is matched with the expenses incurred in earning that revenue.

The **accruals** concept is the fundamental rule about how profits should be calculated. It means that profits are based on revenue and expenses for a time period, whether or not money has been received or paid. It is the reason for many of the special features of final accounts, such as making adjustments for unsold stock and for expenses due or prepaid.

Key terms

Accruals: expenses and revenues are matched for a time period when calculating profit.

Illustration

How to apply the accruals concept

Closing stock: when preparing a trading account it is important to deduct closing stock from the cost of sales. Although this stock will have been paid for during that period, it is really a cost for next period when the goods are sold.

Depreciation: when preparing a profit and loss account it is important to include an estimate of contribution made by each fixed asset to earning the business's sales for that period, even though the payment for the fixed asset will probably have been made several years before.

Expense adjustments: the amount of an expense for a trading period is quite often out of step with the amount actually paid. As a result it is necessary to take account of amounts due but unpaid (accruals), or amounts paid in advance (prepayments) when preparing final accounts.

Background knowledge

The accruals concept is also called the 'matching' concept.

Activity

Laura Kemp is preparing her business's final accounts. She has been advised that she should take account of the following matters:

a an expense has been prepaid

b rent receivable is due but not yet received

c there is a closing stock of unsold goods

d annual depreciation of the business's fixtures and fittings.

In each case explain to Laura in what way she will be applying the accruals concept when taking account of these matters.

Consistency

The **consistency** concept requires businesses to apply the same accounting procedures and policies from one financial period to the next. This ensures that financial statements are prepared in the same way each year. As a result, the users of the financial statements can feel confident that comparisons they make will have some validity.

Case study

Asha Chibuzo applies the consistency concept

Asha Chibuzo owns a business that uses the straight-line method of depreciation. She has been told that this method should be used each year. There should not be a sudden switch to the reducing-balance method of depreciation. Such a change would have a distorting effect on the reported profit for that business for the year in which the change was made, compared to the previous year.

Asha has also been told that if overriding reasons can be found for changing accounting procedures and policies, the consistency rule can be ignored. However, the accounting statements affected by the change should clearly show the effect of the change. Users of the accounts can then make a suitable adjustment when comparing results from one year to the next.

Prudence

Where there is doubt, asset values and profits should be understated rather than overstated. This rule, called the **prudence** concept, ensures that those who have a stake in a business are not misled into thinking that the business is doing better than it really is.

Case study

Hershel applies the prudence concept

Hershel is the owner of a retail business. Hershel's business sold some goods on credit. The amount due has been outstanding from the debtor for some time. All attempts to contact the debtor have failed. Hershel has been prudent and written off the bad debt in the accounts, rather than give an unduly optimistic view of the debtors and profits for the year on the business's balance sheet.

Materiality

The **materiality** concept concerns the treatment of certain items when preparing final accounts and balance sheets. The rule requires that care should be taken to ensure that all information provided is significant to the users of the statements, i.e. it should matter. In other words, trivial items should not be included.

Activity

An individual is looking at the financial results of a limited company for each of the last 3 years. How does that individual benefit from the fact that the limited company's accountant will have applied the consistency concept?

Key terms

Consistency: accounting methods are applied in the same way in each accounting period.

Prudence: where there is doubt, asset and profit values are under- rather than overstated.

Materiality: if the amount involved is relatively insignificant, then the usual accounting treatment of an item can be set aside.

Background knowledge

The prudence concept is sometimes referred to as 'conservatism'.

Case study

Ingrid Magna applies the materiality concept

Ingrid Magna owns a travel agency specialising in winter sports holidays. Ingrid purchased a new paper shredder for use in the office at cost of £80. Ingrid was advised not to record this as a fixed asset, nor subject the item to an annual depreciation charge, on the grounds that it simply would not be worth all the effort to do so. Instead, this minor item of office equipment was written off in that year's profit and loss account.

Realisation

At the heart of the **realisation** concept is the idea that revenue should be recognised when it is certain. In other words a sale should only be included in a business's profit calculations for a financial period if cash has already been paid or there is a promise to pay cash. In practice, a sale is regarded as certain when cash has been paid or an invoice has been issued.

Case study

Lydia French applies the realisation concept

On the last day of the financial year Lydia French notes that her business has cash sales of £8,000, that she has issued invoices to customers totalling £5,000 and that the business has received orders from regular customers totalling £3,000. Lydia records the day's sales as £13,000. Lydia ignores the orders because there is no certainty that they will become definite sales. Lydia might not, for example, be able to fulfil the orders, or the customer might cancel the order.

Business entity

The idea behind the **business entity** concept is that transactions recorded in an organisation's accounts can only relate to that organisation. In other words, transactions relating to the owner's private affairs cannot be recorded in the accounts of the organisation.

Case study

Steve Merritt applies the business entity concept

Steve Merritt is a sole trader. Recently, he used his own resources to pay for a holiday for his family. Steve did not make any record of this transaction in the business's books of account because the transaction did not affect the business.

If Steve had used the business's cash to pay for the holiday, it would be necessary to record the transaction in the business's cash book and drawings account; it would, of course, be incorrect to debit the business's travel expenses account.

Activity

Find out about the policy for writing off low-value fixed assets in the organisation in which you are currently learning/working. In addition, find out about some recent examples of the policy being applied to some low cost items that would otherwise have been regarded as fixed assets.

Background knowledge

Organisations devise their own policy about what should count as material and what value should be regarded as too low in value to warrant recording as a fixed asset. For example, a small organisation might regard expenditure on an asset costing below £500 as an amount to be written off immediately.

Key terms

Realisation: revenue should not be recorded in the accounts until it is realised, i.e. when there is cash or the promise of cash.

Business entity: an accounting system will contain records of that organisation only.

Activity

June Blakey is a sole trader. During the most recently completed financial year the following transactions occurred affecting June and/or her business:

a June took stock from the business's storerooms for her private use, value £400

b June paid her business's electricity bill, £350, from her private resources

c June paid for some kitchen fittings for her family home and paid for these from her personal bank account.

Applying the entity concept, in each case state the double entry, if any, required in the business's books of account to record these transactions.

Applying concepts to stock valuation

Stock valuation provides a good example of how concepts are applied. In particular two concepts feature in an important rule about stock valuation: cost and prudence.

Stock, like any asset, should be valued at cost.

However, the prudence concept states that where there is doubt, asset values should be under- rather than overstated.

Bearing these points in mind consider the following illustrations.

Illustration

How to apply the rule about stock valuation

Denise notes that her business has 20 items in stock that cost £30 each; these items would normally have a selling price of £40 each. Two items are damaged. Denise believes they could be sold at £33 each, but £5 will need to be spent on each of the damaged items in order to put them in a fit state for sale.

Step 1 18 items can be valued at cost £30, total £540

Step 2 Looking carefully at the 2 damaged items the following facts emerge:

- each cost £30

- each could be sold for £33, but in each case the sale at £33 will only take place having spent a further £5, giving a net sale value of £28 per item.

Following the prudence concept, the 2 items should be valued at £28 each (i.e. the net resale value) because it is lower than cost. In other words, where there is doubt, we have under- rather than overvalued items.

The stock will be worth £540 + (2 × £28) i.e. £596.

Some new terms can be used in connection with valuing stocks:

Realisable value – simply means the sale value that can actually be achieved

Net realisable value – means sale value but taking account of any costs that must be incurred before the sale can take place

Key terms

Realisable value: sale value.

Net realisable value: sale value less any costs necessary to incur a sale.

Summary:

The rule that is applied to valuing stocks is as follows:

'stocks must be valued at cost or net realisable value, whichever is lower'.

 Learning outcomes

As a result of studying this chapter, you should now be able to:

- explain the purpose of accounting concepts
- define each of the nine accounting concepts, explain their purpose and give examples of their use.
- explain how accounting concepts are applied to stock valuation
- define terms used in connection with stock valuation such as net realisable value
- calculate stock values based on the application of accounting concepts

Activity

Nimesh, the owner of a retail business, discovered that 20 items in stock that had cost £30 each have been slightly damaged. These items would normally have a selling price of £40 each. However, Nimesh expects that having repackaged each of these items at a cost of £4 each, they can be sold for £31 each. Calculate the total value of these 20 items for inclusion in the business's closing stock.

AQA Examination-style questions

1 (a) Identify which concepts are important when establishing the value of assets.

(b) Identify which concepts are important when assessing profit.

2 ACC3 June 2005

Dimitri sells electrical goods. At his financial year end, he is unsure how to value an electric kettle that he has in stock.

The kettle cost £18. It will sell for £31.

Before it can be sold, the kettle requires a repair which will cost £15.

Required

(a) Calculate the value of the kettle to be included as part of Dimitri's closing stock.

(b) Complete the following sentences.

Stock should be valued at ………………… or ……………………………… whichever is lower. This is an example of using the …………………… concept.

3 ACC3 January 2005

(a) Daniel has included £720 sales to Bill Brown in October 2007 in the total sales for the year ended 31 December 2007. Bill has yet to pay for the goods.

This is an example of the …………………………… concept.

(b) Daniel owns a delivery van that belonged to his grandfather and has great sentimental value. He recently refused an offer of £4,000 for it from a heritage museum. Daniel shows the van on his balance sheet at cost £650.

This is an example of the …………………………… concept.

4 ACC3 June 2004

Explain the usefulness of applying accounting principles and concepts when preparing a set of final accounts for a business.

7

Final accounts and balance sheets of sole traders

In this chapter you will be able to develop your skills in preparing the final accounts of sole traders. You will be able to build on the techniques you learnt in Unit 1 where you prepared basic trading accounts, profit and loss account and balance sheets. You will find that your understanding of how expense items are adjusted for prepayments and amounts due can now be applied to income items. You will develop your knowledge of depreciation and learn how it is recorded in ledger accounts as well as in the final accounts. This chapter will introduce you to some more sophisticated techniques that are designed to ensure that the important task of calculating profits is carried out in a systematic and fair way to properly reflect a business's performance. You will learn how to reduce a business's profits based on an estimate of amounts that will be lost in future because some debtors are unlikely to pay. You will also learn how to distinguish between two types of expenditure (revenue and capital) that will be important if you are to produce accurate profit calculations. All these new techniques will also be of value when you prepare the final accounts and balance sheets of other organisations such as limited companies.

Link

- You will study limited companies in Chapter 8
- You will study partnerships in A2 Accounting Unit 3

1 Bad debts recovered and income received in advance and due

In this topic you will learn:

- how to explain the term 'bad debts recovered'
- how to explain potential sources of income for a sole trader
- how to record bad debts recovered in ledger accounts and in final accounts
- how to record adjustments for income received in advance when preparing final accounts

Bad debts recovered

What is a bad debt recovered?

When a debtor cannot pay the amount due because of bankruptcy, the account is written off as a bad debt. Sometimes a debtor will pay the amount due after a business has written off the debtor's account as a bad debt. The amount is recorded as a **'bad debt recovered'**. The recovery of a bad debt is, of course, good news for a business.

How is a bad debt recovered recorded?

Step 1: Reinstate the debtor's account:

Dr Debtor

Cr Bad Debts Recovered

Step 2: Record the amount received from the debtor

Dr Bank Account

Cr Debtor

The balance of a bad debt recovered account is subsequently transferred to the profit and loss account at the business's year end. The amount will be **recorded as a gain** in the **profit and loss account**.

Case study

Murray Traders

Jim Murray is the owner of a wholesale business called Murray Traders. The business sells clothes and footwear for the young adult market. As a wholesaler the business has many credit customers ranging from small retail shops to some of the larger well-known chains. The business owns extensive freehold premises part of which has been sublet to a tenant. In recent years, Jim Murray has invested the business's surplus cash in a number of investments.

Illustration

How to record a bad debts recovered in the ledger accounts

On 12 February a business, Murray Traders, received a cheque from Tom Scott for £1,840. Tom Scott had owed the business this sum, but his account had been written off as a bad debt six months previously.

Record this information is the business's books of account. Show how this information would be recorded in the business's trial balance, bad debts recovered account, and profit and loss account.

- how to record adjustments for income due when preparing final accounts
- how to record entries for adjustments to income in ledger accounts
- how to record income account balances on balance sheets.

Link

For more information on bad debts, see Chapter 4, page 62.

Key terms

Bad debt recovered: an amount received from a debtor that has previously been written off.

Income received in advance: money received by a business from a debtor (such as a tenant) but that relates to the next financial period.

Dr			Debtor: Tom Scott			Cr
Feb 12	Bad debts recovered	580	Feb 12	Bank		580

Dr				Cash Book (extract)			Cr
		Cash	Bank	Cash			Bank
Feb 12	Debtor: Tom Scott		580				

Dr			Bad Debts Recovered Account			Cr
Dec 31	Profit and loss	1,840	Feb 12	Tom Scott		1,840

Trial Balance (extract) at 31 December 2007		
	Dr	Cr
	£	£
Bad debts recovered		1,840

Activity

Jim Murray, the owner of 'Murray Traders' has just received a cheque from another debtor, Sarah Cameron, for £320. Sarah's account had been written off several years ago as a bad debt. Explain to Jim Murray how this bad debt recovered should be treated when preparing a profit and loss account?

Profit and Loss Account (Extract)
for the year ended 31 December 2007

		£	£
Gross Profit			184,500
Add	**Bad debt recovered**		**1,840**
			186,340
Less	Business rates	11,450	
	Insurance etc.	3,720	

Figure 7.1 *How to record a bad debts recovered*

Income received in advance

What is income received in advance?

Taking rent receivable as an example of income received in advance, it is possible for a tenant to pay rent in advance. If the rent is received for a period stretching into the next financial year, it will be necessary to adjust the amount to be recorded in the profit and loss account, so that it records rent receivable only for this financial year.

Rent receivable received in advance is a **current liability**.

Illustration

How to record income received in advance

Murray Traders sublets part of its premises. The business had received a total of £3900 from its tenant for rent during the year ended 31 December 2007. This amount includes a payment for one month's rent of £300 for January 2008.

How would this information be recorded in the business's rent receivable account? Show how rent receivable will appear in the trial balance, profit and loss account for the year ended 31 December 2007 and balance sheet at 31 December 2007.

Step 1: record the receipt of £3,900 in the rent receivable account

Step 2: transfer the appropriate amount to the profit and loss

Step 3: balance the account

Dr			Rent Receivable Account					Cr
Dec	31	Profit and loss	3600	Dec	31	Total receipts	3,900
	31	Balance c/d	300				
			3900				3,900
				Jan	1	Balance b/d	300

Trial balance entry

Trial Balance (Extract) at
31 December 2007

	Dr	Cr
	£	£
Rent receivable		3,900

Profit and loss account entry

Profit and Loss Account (Extract)
for the year ended 31 December 2007

	£	£
Gross Profit		83,780
Add: rent receivable		
(£3900–£300)		**3,600**
		87,380
Less: advertising	4,500	
bank charges	670	
etc.		

Balance sheet entry

Balance Sheet (Extract) at 31 December 2007

Current liabilities	£
Rent received in advance	300

Figure 7.2 *Recording income received in advance*

Income due

What is income due?

Taking interest receivable as an example of **income due**, frequently the dates when interest is received by a business will not match the business's financial period. It is possible, therefore, that at the end of a financial year interest may still be due on savings or an investment, but will not actually be received until the next financial period.

Illustration

How to record income due

Murray Traders has received £4,800 in interest on an investment account during the year ended 31 December 2007. At 31 December 2006 interest £420 is due but not yet received.

How should this information be recorded in the Interest Received Account? Show how interest received should be recorded in the trial balance, profit and loss account for the year ended 31 December 2007 and balance sheet at 31 December 2007.

Activity

Murray Traders has received interest of £4,100 during a financial period. However, £250 of this amount relates to the next financial year. Explain to Jim Murray how much interest received should be transferred to the profit and loss account for this financial period.

Key terms

Income due: money that should have been received by a business from a debtor (such as a tenant) relating to the current financial period but that is yet to be received.

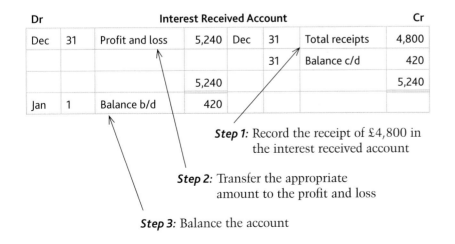

Dr		Interest Received Account					Cr
Dec	31	Profit and loss	5,240	Dec	31	Total receipts	4,800
					31	Balance c/d	420
			5,240				5,240
Jan	1	Balance b/d	420				

Step 1: Record the receipt of £4,800 in the interest received account

Step 2: Transfer the appropriate amount to the profit and loss

Step 3: Balance the account

Trial balance entry

Trial Balance (Extract) at 31 December 2007

	Dr	Cr
	£	£
Interest received		4,800

Profit and loss account entry

Profit and Loss Account (Extract)
for the year ended 31 December 2007

	£	£
Gross Profit		154,000
Add: interest received		
(£4800+£420)		**5,240**
		159,240
Less: business rates	9,200	
carriage outwards etc	3,220	

Balance sheet entry

Balance Sheet at 31 December 2007 (Extract)

Current assets	£
Interest received due	420

Figure 7.3 *Recording income due*

Background knowledge

Making adjustments in income accounts is another example of the application of the accruals concept.

Activity

Explain to Jim Murray why income due is shown as a current asset on a balance sheet.

 *Learning outcomes*

As a result of studying this topic, you should now be able to:

- define bad debts recovered, income received in advance and income due
- record these items in ledger accounts
- prepare final accounts of a sole trader that include bad debts recovered and adjustments for income received in advance and due
- record income received and advance and income due on a balance sheet

AQA Examiner's tip

It is important to show workings when answering examination questions. So if you have to adjust income, show details of how you reached the figure to be shown in the profit and loss account.

AQA Examination-style questions

1 The final accounts of a sole trader's business are being prepared for the year ended 31 December 2007. The following information is available concerning three income items. Calculate the amount to be shown in the business's profit and loss account for the year under review.

	Amount received during year ended 31 December 2007	Additional information at 31 December 2007	Amount to be entered in Profit and Loss for year ended 31 December 2007
Interest receivable	£4,700	Interest £450 is due but not yet received	£ ....
Commission receivable	£11,490	Commission £620 is received in advance	£ ....
Rent receivable	£16,320	One tenant has paid rent £560 in advance for 2007; a second tenant owes £830 for 2007	£ ....

2   A business received rent from a tenant. During the year ended 31 March 2008, the tenant had paid £9,800 in rent. This amount includes rent of £1,400 for April and May 2008.

Complete the rent receivable account to record all these details. Include an entry to transfer rent receivable for the year to the profit and loss account. Balance the account.

Dr			Rent Receivable Account			Cr

3   A business receives interest at a fixed rate of 6% per annum on an investment of £18,000. During the year ended 31 December 2007 the business had received 10 months' rent, with rent for November and December due but not yet received.

Make entries in the interest received account for the year ended 31 December 2007 to record this information. Include an entry to transfer interest receivable for the year to the profit and loss account. Balance the account.

Dr			Interest Receivable Account			Cr

4   Carol Andrews owns a retail business. On 31 December 2007 the following trial balance was extracted from the accounts of the business after the preparation of the trading account for the year ended 31 December 2007.

Additional information at 31 December 2007

Trial Balance at 31 December 2007	Dr £	Cr £
Advertising	826	
Bad debt recovered		119
Bad debts written off	286	
Business rates	11,294	
Capital		410,000
Carriage outwards	208	
Cash at bank	5,772	
Cash in hand	399	
Commission receivable		2,820
Drawings	38,540	
Freehold Premises at cost	380,000	
Gross profit for year		135,000
Insurance	3,986	
Light and heat	1,293	
Rent Receivable		4,850
Shop furniture and fittings		
cost	45,000	
provision for depreciation		9,000
Stock, 31 December 2007	29,552	
Trade creditors		22,418
Trade debtors	18,311	
Wages and salaries	48,740	
	584,207	584,207

1   Business rates £340 is due and insurance £411 is prepaid.
2   Commission receivable £140 is due but not yet received; rent receivable £490 has been received in advance.
3   Depreciation should be provided on shop furniture and fittings at 20% per annum using the straight-line method.

Prepare a profit and loss account for the year ended 31 December 2007 and a balance sheet at that date.

2   Provisions for doubtful debts

☑ Creating a provision for doubtful debts

Why create a provision for doubtful debts?

Businesses have a duty to present a '**true and fair view**' of their affairs. It follows that if a business tends to have bad debts, it should consider reducing the value of its trade debtors when preparing a balance sheet to reflect the fact that it is likely that some of the amount shown as due will not be received. This idea of presenting a *fair* view of trade debtors on a balance sheet leads to the creation of what is called a **provision for doubtful debts**. A provision for doubtful debts is a good example of the application of the prudence concept.

The amount of the provision for doubtful debts is often based on recent experience of the amount of bad debts in relation to total credit sales.

How to create a provision for doubtful debts

The entries required to create a provision for doubtful debts are:

Debit Profit and Loss Account

Credit Provision for Doubtful Debts Account

¹²₃ Illustration

How to create a provision for doubtful debts

Murray Traders has regularly experienced bad debts. On 31 December 2005, the total of trade debtors as shown in the business's sales ledger was £24,000. Based on recent experience, the owner of the business has decided to create a provision for doubtful debts of 5% of trade debtors at the year end.

Record the creation of the provision for doubtful debts in the books of Murray Traders:

Step 1: Calculate the provision: 5% of trade debtors £24,000 = £1,200.

Dr			Provision for Doubtful Debts Account			Cr
		Dec	31	Profit and loss		1,200

Profit and Loss Account (Summary)
for the year ended 31 December 2005

	£	£
Gross Profit		120,000
Less: expenses	47,000	
depreciation	13,000	
provision for doubtful debts	**1,200**	
		61,200
Net Profit		58,800

Balance Sheet as at 31 December 2005 (Extract)

	£	£
CURRENT ASSETS		
Trade debtors	24,000	
Less provision for doubtful debts	1,200	
		22,800

Figure 7.4 *Creating a provision for doubtful debts*

In this topic you will learn:

- why businesses create provisions for doubtful debts

- under what circumstances it would be necessary to increase or decrease a provision for doubtful debts

- how to record a provision for doubtful debts in the general ledger and in the final accounts and balance sheet

- how to record a change in the provision for doubtful debts in the general ledger and in the final accounts.

Key terms

True and fair view: the principle that accounting records should be factually accurate wherever this is possible, or otherwise present a reasonable estimate of, or judgement about, the financial position.

Provision for doubtful debts: an amount set aside from profits to take account of the likelihood that some debtors will not be able to pay the amount due.

Step 2: Open a provision for doubtful debts account (in the business's general ledger) and make a credit entry for the provision

Step 3: Make a matching debit entry in the profit and loss account

Step 4: Ensure that when trade debtors are recorded on the balance sheet, they are reduced by the amount of the provision

Activity

Jim Murray has just created a provision for doubtful debts account. However, he says he does not really understand why the account has a credit balance. Explain why a provision for doubtful debts account has a credit balances.

■ Increasing a provision for doubtful debts

When should a business increase its provision for doubtful debts?

Once a provision for doubtful debts is created it remains in the accounting system, but it is reviewed annually. If there is an increase in the total of trade debtors at the year end, then the provision should be increased to keep in step with this change.

The entries required to increase a provision for doubtful debts are:

Debit Profit and Loss Account *with the amount of the increase*

Credit Provision for Doubtful Debts Account *with the amount of the increase*

■ Illustration

How to increase a provision for doubtful debts

At 31 December 2006 the total of trade debtors in Murray Traders' sales ledger was £28,000. Jim Murray requires the provision for doubtful debts to be maintained at 5% of trade debtors.

Make entries to maintain the provision for doubtful debts at 5% of trade debtors.

Step 1: Calculate the amount of the revised provision for doubtful debts: 5% × £28,000 = £1,400

Step 2: Calculate the amount by which the existing provision needs to be changed

The existing provision is £1,200 so it will be necessary to add a further £200 to achieve the revised figure of £1,400.

Step 3: Make an entry to alter the existing provision in the provision for doubtful debts account

Step 4: Balance the provision account to show the revised figure for the provision

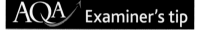

Dr				Provision for Doubtful Debts Account				Cr
2006				**2005**				
Dec	31	Balance c/d	1,400	Dec	31	Profit and loss	1,200	
				2006				
				Dec	31	Profit and loss	200	
			1,400					**1,400**
				Dec	31	Balance b/d	1,400	

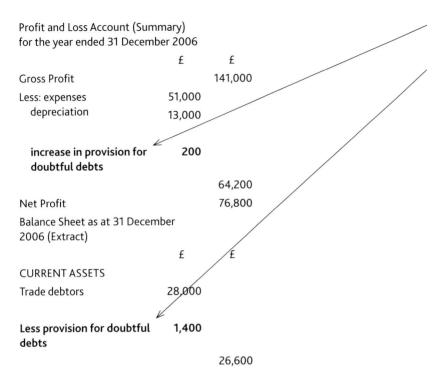

Profit and Loss Account (Summary)
for the year ended 31 December 2006

	£	£
Gross Profit		141,000
Less: expenses	51,000	
depreciation	13,000	
increase in provision for doubtful debts	**200**	
		64,200
Net Profit		76,800

Balance Sheet as at 31 December 2006 (Extract)

	£	£
CURRENT ASSETS		
Trade debtors	28,000	
Less provision for doubtful debts	**1,400**	
		26,600

Step 5: Make a matching entry in the profit and loss account

Step 6: Ensure that when the balance sheet is prepared the updated balance on the provision for doubtful debts account is deducted from trade debtors

Figure 7.5 *Recording an increase in a provision*

Decreasing a provision for doubtful debts

When should a business decrease a provision for doubtful debts?

The total of trade debtors could decrease from one year to the next. In this situation the amount of the provision for doubtful debts should be decreased to keep in step with the decrease in trade debtors.

How should a business decrease its provision for doubtful debts?

The entries required to decrease a provision for doubtful debts are:

Debit Provision for Doubtful
Debts Account   *with the amount of the decrease*

Credit Profit and Loss Account   *with the amount of the decrease*

Illustration

How to decrease a provision for doubtful debts

At 31 December 2007 the total of trade debtors in Murray Traders' sales ledger is £22,000. Jim Murray requires the provision for doubtful debts to be maintained at 5% of trade debtors.

Step 1: Calculate the amount of the revised provision for doubtful debts: 5% × £22,00 = £1,100

Step 2: Calculate the amount by which the existing provision needs to be changed

The existing provision is £1,400 so it will be necessary to decrease the provision by £300 to arrive at the revised balance of £1,100.

Activity

A business already has a provision for doubtful debts of £1,100. At the end the financial period the provision for doubtful debts is to be maintained at 2.5% of trade debtors, which total £48,000. By how much should the provision for doubtful debts be increased? State the double entry necessary to increase the provision for doubtful debts.

Activity

A business has a provision for doubtful debts of £480. At the end of its financial year, the business has trade debtors of £12,800. The provision for doubtful debts is to be maintained as 5% of trade debtors. By how much should the provision for doubtful debts be decreased? State the double entry necessary to reduce the provision for doubtful debts

Dr								Provision for Doubtful Debts Account								Cr
2006						2005					
Dec	31	Balance c/d	1,400			Dec	31	Profit and loss	1,200
						2006			
						Dec	31	Profit and loss	200
			1,400						1,400
2007						Dec	31	Balance b/d	1,400
Dec	31	Profit and loss	300						
	31	Balance c/d	1,100						
			1,400						1,400
						Dec	31	Balance b/d	1,100

Step 3: Make an entry to alter the existing provision in the provision for doubtful debts account

Step 4: Balance the provision account to show the revised figure for the provision

Profit and Loss Account (Summary)
for the year ended 31 December 2007

	£	£
Gross Profit		152,000
Add: decrease in provision for doubtful debts		**300**
		152,300
Less: expenses	57,000	
depreciation	13,000	
		70,000
Net Profit		82,300

Step 5: Make a matching entry in the profit and loss account

Balance Sheet as at 31 December 2007 (Extract)

	£	£
CURRENT ASSETS		
Trade debtors	22,000	
Less provision for doubtful debts	1,100	
		20,900

Step 6: Ensure that when the balance sheet is prepared the updated balance on the provision for doubtful debts account is deducted from trade debtors

Figure 7.6 *Recording a decrease in a provision*

🔍✅ *Learning outcomes*

As a result of studying this topic, you should now be able to:

- define the term provision for doubtful debts
- explain why businesses create provisions for doubtful debts
- record provisions for doubtful debts in ledger accounts
- prepare final accounts that include the creation of a provision for doubtful debts or an adjustment to an existing provision for doubtful debts
- record a provision for doubtful debts on a balance sheet

 Examination-style questions

1 The owner of a business decided to introduce a provision for doubtful debts. It was agreed that the provision should be maintained at 5% of trade debtors at each year end.

Trade debtors at 31 December:

Year 1 £18,400

Year 2 £17,600

Year 3 £19,600

Complete the following table recording information about this business's provision for doubtful debts.

Year	Provision for Doubtful Debts £	Amount to be entered in Profit and Loss Account £	Entry in Provision for Doubtful Debts Account (enter debit or credit)
1			
2			
3			

2 A business maintains a provision for doubtful debts accounts. The policy is to maintain the provision at 2.5% of trade debtors at each year end. On 31 December 2005, the balance on this account was £850.

Trade debtors at 31 December were:

	£
2006	38,600
2007	35,000

Prepare the provision for doubtful debts account showing entries for the three years 2005, 2006 and 2007. The account should be balanced on 31 December 2006 and 31 December 2007.

Dr								Cr

Provision for Doubtful Debts Account

AQA Examiner's tip

The most common error with provisions for doubtful debts is for candidates to forget that a provision already exists. As a result, while it is necessary only to add or deduct a small adjusting amount, some candidates tend to make entries in the profit and loss account for the whole provision.

AQA Examiner's tip

When preparing final accounts, check what the situation is in regard to a provision for doubtful debts.

- Is there an existing provision (if so, it will appear in the end of year trial balance), or are you to create a provision for the first time?

- If there is already a provision, should it be increased or decreased? (Remember, it is only the amount of the increase or decrease that should be shown in the profit and loss account.)

3   Alison Redman owns a retail business. The financial year ends on 31 December 2007. On this date the following trial balance was extracted from the books of the business.

Trial Balance
at 31 December 2007

	Dr £	Cr £
Bad debts	428	
Bank overdraft		3,962
Business rates	9,910	
Capital		115,000
Carriage inwards	1,190	
Discounts allowed	322	
Discounts received		189
Drawings	27,488	
Fixed assets		
cost	160,000	
provision for depreciation 1 January 2007		64,000
Insurance	3,674	
Provision for doubtful debts 1 January 2007		990
Purchases	152,498	
Sales		262,581
Stock 1 January 2007	18,450	
Trade creditors		13,244
Trade debtors	17,800	
Wages and salaries	68,206	
	459,966	459,966

Additional information at 31 December 2007

1   Stocks were valued at £22,320.

2   Wages and salaries £2,390 was due; business rates £280 was prepaid.

3   Depreciation on fixed assets should be provided at 20% per annum using the straight-line method.

4   The provision for doubtful debts should be maintained at 5% of trade debtors.

Required

(a)   Prepare the trading and profit and loss account for the year ended 31 December 2007.

(b)   Prepare a balance sheet at 31 December 2007.

3 Depreciation

AQA Examiner's tip

Try to remember to use some of these technical expressions (such as 'useful economic life') when writing about depreciation.

Key terms

Depreciation: the loss in value of a fixed asset over its useful economic life that is apportioned to financial periods. It is a non-cash expense.

Straight-line method: where the annual depreciation charge is based on the cost of the fixed asset.

Reducing-balance method: where the annual depreciation charge is based on the net book value of the fixed asset at the beginning of each financial period.

Links

The straight-line method can be seen in Chapter 4, pages 61–62

💡 ✅ Understanding and recording depreciation

Why do businesses depreciate fixed assets?

Almost all fixed assets have what is called a useful economic life. This means there is a limited amount of time during which the fixed asset will be of value to a business. The useful life of an asset is limited for a variety of reasons:

- assets lose value as they are used, that is they are subject to wear and tear (example vehicles, buildings)

- some assets are likely to become obsolete due to the pace of technological change; that is cease to be up to date and therefore unable to meet the needs of a business (example office equipment such as computers)

- alternatively, some assets might become inadequate, that is fail to meet the needs of the business because they have limited capacity and the business has grown in size (example, office equipment such as a photocopier)

- some assets' life has a legal limit and becomes valueless at the end of that time (example, the lease of shop premises)

Land is the only obvious exception to the rule that fixed assets should be depreciated. Land is assumed to have an indefinite life.

Depreciation is the means by which the loss in value of a fixed asset is spread out over the useful life of the asset. Depreciation is an expense. It is an example of the application of the accruals concept and ensures that the cost of an asset is matched to the income the asset creates in a financial period.

How is depreciated calculated using the reducing-balance method of depreciation?

As well as the **straight-line method** of depreciation, it is also possible to calculate depreciation basing the annual charge on the net book value of the asset as the beginning of the year, rather than its original cost. This alternative method is called the **reducing-balance method**.

Illustration

How to calculate depreciation using the reducing-balance method

Murray Traders owns a motor vehicle that was purchased on 1 January 2005 for £18,000. It is the policy of the business to depreciate motor vehicles by 20% per annum using the reducing-balance method.

■ Link

For more information on depreciation, see Chapter 4, page 61.

Calculate the depreciation charge on the motor vehicle for each of the years ended 31 December 2005, 2006 and 2007.

	Value of asset at beginning of year £	Depreciation calculation £	Depreciation charge £
2005	18,000	20% × £18,000	3,600
2006	14,400	20% × £14,400	2,880
2007	11,520	20% × £11,520	2,304

Table 7.1 *Calculating depreciation*

Activity

A business has a fixed asset that cost £100,000. If depreciation is provided annually at 20% using the reducing-balance method, calculate the depreciation charge in year 2.

How do the two methods of depreciation compare?

The straight-line method of depreciation:

■ is straightforward to calculate

■ results in an even depreciation charge each year.

The reducing-balance method of depreciation:

■ is more complex to calculate

■ results in a declining depreciation charge from one year to the next, which may reflect reality for certain assets

■ may result in a more even charge against profits each year for fixed assets if maintenance, repairs and servicing charges are considered alongside depreciation.

How to record depreciation in the ledger

Businesses keep separate records of the cost of each type of fixed asset and the accumulating depreciation on each type of fixed asset. So in the general ledger you are likely to find, for example, the following two accounts:

Machinery (at cost) Account

Provision for Depreciation of Machinery Account

At the end of each financial year the provision for depreciation account is updated with the annual depreciation charge. The double entry is as follows:

Dr Profit and Loss Account

Cr Provision for Depreciation Account

As a result the amount recorded in provision for depreciation account accumulates as the years go by, until the fixed asset is sold or scrapped.

Illustration

How to record depreciation in ledger accounts

Murray Traders purchased some machinery on 1 January 2005 for £50,000. Machinery is depreciated by 20% per annum using the straight-line method.

Record this information in the business's general ledger for the years 2005, 2006 and 2007.

Step 1: Calculate the annual depreciation charge: 20% × cost £50,000, i.e. £10,000

Step 2: Prepare two separate accounts for machinery in the general ledger

Step 3: Record the purchase of machinery on 1 January 2005

Dr			Machinery at Cost Account				Cr
2005							
Jan	1	Bank	50,000				

Dr			Provision for Depreciation (Machinery) Account				Cr
2006				2005			
Dec	31	Balance c/d	20,000	Dec	31	Profit and loss	10,000
				2006			
				Dec	31	Profit and loss	10,000
			20,000	2007			20,000
2007				Jan	1	Balance b/d	20,000
Dec	31	Balance c/d	30,000	Dec	31	Profit and loss	10,000
			30,000				30,000
				2008			
				Jan	1	Balance b/d	30,000

Figure 7.10 *Recording depreciation in the ledger*

Step 4: Record the first year's depreciation charge on 31 December 2005

Step 5: Record the depreciation charge for the year ended 31 December 2006 and balance the provision account

Step 6: Record the depreciation charge for the year ended 31 December 2007 and balance the provision account

Activity

Does a provision for depreciation account have a debit or credit balance?

The Sale of a Fixed Asset

How to record the sale of a fixed asset

When a fixed asset is sold, it will be necessary to:

- eliminate the original cost of the fixed assets from the ledger;
- eliminate the accumulated depreciation on that fixed asset;
- record the amount received for the fixed asset in the sale;
- assess whether a profit or loss was made on the sale of the asset.

The process involves the use of a 'fixed asset disposal account'. This account will automatically show the profit or loss made on the sale as the closing balance of the account. A profit will arise if the asset is sold for more than its net book value; a loss will arise if the asset is sold for less than its net book value. The profit or loss on disposal is transferred to the business's profit and loss account as a gain or a loss at the end of the financial period.

Illustration

How to record the sale of a fixed asset

Murray Traders purchased some office equipment on 1 January 2005 for £12,000. The office equipment was depreciated by 25% per annum using the straight-line method on 31 December 2005 and 31 December 2006. The accounts recording this information are shown opposite.

On 17 May 2007 the office equipment was sold for £2,300 and a cheque received for this amount.

Record the disposal of the fixed asset in the business's ledger.

Step 1: Prepare an Office Equipment Disposal Account

Step 2: Transfer the cost of the office equipment to the disposal account

Step 3: Transfer the accumulated depreciation charge to the disposal account

Step 4: Record the receipt of the cheque in the disposal account

Step 5: Balance the disposal account. The balance will show automatically whether there is a loss or profit on the disposal that is transferred to the profit and loss account.

Dr			Office Equipment at Cost				Cr
2005				2007			
Jan	1	Bank	12,000	May	17	Disposal	12,000

Dr			Provision For Depreciation (Office Equipment) Account				Cr
2006				2005			
Dec	31	Balance c/d	6,000	Dec	31	Profit and loss	3,000
				2006			
				Dec	31	Profit and loss	3,000
			6,000				6,000
2007				2007			
May	17	Disposal	6,000	Jan	1	Balance b/d	6,000

Dr			Office Equipment Disposal Account				Cr
2007				2007			
May	17	Disposal	12,000	May	17	Depreciation	6,000
					17	Bank	2,300
					17	P&L (loss)	3,700
			12,000				12,000

Figure 7.11 *Recording the sale of a fixed asset*

Note: the loss will be recorded in the profit and loss account as an extra cost for the year.

Activity

If a business made a profit on the disposal of a fixed asset, would the amount of the loss appear as a debit or credit entry in the asset disposal account?

AQA Examiner's tip

- Don't forget to set out your workings for depreciation calculations.

- Some candidates fail to read the information provided carefully and use the wrong method for calculating depreciation. Always check whether you are to use the straight-line or reducing-balance method.

✓💡 Learning outcomes

As a result of studying this topic, you should now be able to:

- define the key term depreciation

- explain why businesses depreciate their fixed assets

- calculate depreciation using both the straight-line and reducing-balance methods

- evaluate the two methods of calculating depreciation

- prepare a provision for depreciation account recording entries for depreciation over several years

- prepare a ledger account to record the disposal of a fixed asset

- prepare final accounts that include depreciation of fixed assets and the profit or loss on the disposal of a fixed asset
- prepare balance sheets showing information about fixed assets: cost, accumulated depreciation and net book value

 Examination-style questions

☑ 1 The following information is available about a business's fixed assets.

Fixed asset	Cost £	Depreciation Rate	Depreciation Method
Freehold Premises	340,000	2% per annum	Straight line
Motor Vehicles	60,000	30% per annum	Reducing balance

Calculate the depreciation charge on each fixed asset for Year 2.

2 On 1 January 2005 a business acquired some machinery at a cost of £36,000. The business's policy is to depreciate machinery by 40% per annum using the reducing-balance method. The business's accounting year end is 31 December.

Prepare the provision for depreciation of machinery account in the business's ledger for each of the three years 2005, 2006 and 2007.

Dr		Provision for Depreciation (Machinery) Account					Cr

3 A business sold a motor vehicle on 19 March 2007. The vehicle had been purchased for £15,300 and had a net book value of £5,800 at the date of disposal. A cheque for £6,500 was received for the vehicle on the date of sale.

Prepare the motor vehicle disposal account in the business's ledger.

 **Examiner's tip**

Remember to balance the depreciation account at the end of 2006 and again at the end of 2007.

Dr		Motor Vehicle Disposal Account					Cr

4   Danny Forsyth owns a bookshop called 'The Bookshelf'. His most recent financial year ended on 31 March 2008. A trial balance was extracted from the business's books at this date after the preparation of the trading account for the year.

Trial Balance at 31 March 2008	Dr £	Cr £
Administration expenses	8,437	
Bank loan (repayable June 2008)		8,000
Bank loan interest	683	
Business rates	9,300	
Capital		262,700
Carriage outwards	478	
Cash at bank	1,905	
Cash in hand	36	
Delivery vehicle		
cost	16,400	
provision for depreciation 1 April 2007		4,100
Drawings	28,331	
Fixtures and fittings		
cost	15,300	
provision for depreciation 1 April 2007		3,060
Freehold Premises		
cost	260,000	
provision for depreciation 1 April 2007		26,000
Gross Profit		86,370
Light and heat	3,698	
Loss on sale of fixtures and fittings	395	
Shop assistants' wages	33,209	
Stock at 31 March 2008	24,725	
Trade creditors		14,987
Trade debtors	2,320	
	405,217	405,217

Additional information at 31 March 2008

■ Light and heat £164 was due but unpaid; administration expenses £311 was prepaid.

■ The business's depreciation policies are as follows:

	rate per annum %	method
Delivery vehicle	25	reducing balance
Fixtures and fittings	20	straight line
Freehold premises	2	straight line

Required

(a)   Prepare the profit and loss account for the year ended 31 March 2008.

(b)   Prepare a balance sheet at 31 March 2008.

4   Capital and revenue expenditure

Key terms

Capital expenditure: money spent on fixed assets that is intended to benefit future financial periods.

Revenue expenditure: money spent on running costs that benefits only the current financial period.

Understanding the terms revenue and capital expenditure

What is capital expenditure?

Put simply, **capital expenditure** is money spent on fixed assets.

A more sophisticated definition would mention that it is money spent that has a long-term benefit to a business.

Long term means more than one year.

Examples of capital expenditure:

The purchase of any fixed asset such as premises, machinery, equipment, vehicles, fixtures, fittings.

Money spent improving the fixed asset that adds value to the fixed asset, such as fitting storage racks to a delivery van, or decorating (as opposed to redecorating) a newly built extension to an office block.

Capital expenditure also includes money spent on acquiring fixed assets or making them available for use. Examples include: legal costs when purchasing premises, carriage costs when purchasing new office equipment, installation costs when installing a new machine. In each of these situations the argument is that the benefit from spending money on these costs is as long lasting as the fixed asset itself.

What is revenue expenditure?

Revenue expenditure refers to money spent on running costs. A more sophisticated definition would mention that it is money spent that has short-term benefit to a business, where short-term means less than one year. A feature of revenue expenditure is that it is recurring, i.e. has to be paid for again and again.

Examples of revenue expenditure:

Any expense such as wages, salaries, light and heat, rent, rates, insurance, etc.

Repairs, renewals, maintenance and servicing costs are also considered to be revenue expenditure. The argument is that these costs do not add any value to the fixed asset.

Applying the terms

Illustration

How to distinguish between revenue and capital expenditure
Murray Traders purchased a new delivery van. The following payments were made when the delivery van was purchased.

	£
Delivery van	17,400
Insurance of van	860
Adapting shelving to create more storage space	520
First tank of fuel	30
Road fund licence	160
Painting "Murray Traders" and the business logo on sides of van	220

Table 7.2 *Delivery van payments*

Activity

Jim Murray has recently purchased some new equipment for Murray Traders. He has been told that the amount paid in wages to an employee who installed the new equipment should be added to the value of the equipment. Jim says he thought wages were an expense that was recorded in the profit and loss account. Explain to Jim why, in this situation, wages should be added to the value of the equipment.

Calculate the total revenue expenditure and total capital expenditure.

Capital items are: delivery van; adapting shelving; painting name and logo

Revenue items are: insurance; fuel, road fund licence

Capital: £17,400 + £520 + £220 = £18,140

Revenue: £860 + £30 + £160 = £1,050

Note: it follows from this calculation that the delivery van account should record £18,140 as the cost of the van and the annual depreciation charge should be based on this amount. The revenue expenditure of £1,050 should be charged to the profit and loss account at the end of the financial period.

AQA Examiner's tip

The most common error with this topic is to mix up the definitions. To avoid this problem, find some way of linking capital expenditure with fixed assets, and revenue expenditure with running costs.

The importance of the distinction

Why does the distinction between capital and revenue expenditure matter?

Expenditure regarded as capital expenditure affects the figures shown for fixed assets on a balance sheet.

Expenditure regarded as revenue expenditure affects the figures shown for expenses in a business's profit and loss account.

If errors are made in classifying expenditure, it follows that fixed asset totals and net profits figures will be inaccurate. If net profit is inaccurate, the figure for capital on the balance sheet will also be inaccurate.

Fixed assets totals, net profit and capital figures are all important for the managers or owners of businesses when analysing business performance. If the analysis is based on inaccurate information, it is likely that the managers or owners will draw incorrect conclusions and possibly make wrong decisions.

Learning outcomes

As a result of studying this topic, you should now be able to:

- explain the meaning of each of the terms capital and revenue expenditure and give examples of each
- apply your understanding of these terms to a variety of different situations
- calculate figures for total revenue and capital expenditure correctly selecting items from a list

- explain why the distinction between the two terms is important in preparing financial statements
- prepare final accounts and balance sheets that reflect the correct treatment of items of revenue and capital expenditure

 Examination-style questions

1 Define the terms:
  - revenue expenditure
  - capital expenditure.

  Give one example of each type of expenditure.

 Examiner's tip

In your answer to Question 3 don't forget to show detailed workings.

2 In each of the following examples, state whether the amount spent is revenue expenditure or capital expenditure. Assume the business trades in groceries.

	Expenditure	Type of expenditure: capital or revenue
a	Advertising a special sale event	
b	New office furniture	
c	Maintenance of photocopier	
d	Improvements to staff rest room	
e	Estate agent's fees on purchase of new premises	
f	Redecoration of manager's office	

3 The Sales Director of a well-known chain of newsagents has recently had a new computer system installed in her office.

The total expenditure involved was as follows:

	£
Computer hardware	1,200
Stock of paper	40
Extra memory for computer	120
Printer	300
Printer cartridges	30
Computer software	360
Air-conditioning unit	450

Calculate the total capital expenditure and total revenue expenditure.

Limited liability companies are a particularly important form of organisation because so many larger businesses in the UK are limited companies, and, as a result, a very significant amount of business activity in the British economy is conducted by this form of organisation. Many businesses that are familiar names to everyone are limited companies, including leading retailers such as Marks and Spencer plc and Littlewoods Ltd, manufacturers such as Cadbury Schweppes plc, world-famous football clubs, such as Manchester United plc, and fast food chains, such as McDonald's UK, etc. In Chapter 5 you will already have learned about the advantages and disadvantages of forming a limited company. In this chapter you will learn about the more practical aspects of preparing the accounts of a limited company. You will find that many of the skills you have developed when preparing a sole trader's final accounts will be very useful as the basis of the work you are going to do on limited companies. For example, a limited company's trading and profit and loss account is very similar to that of a sole trader; the assets and liabilities that are to be found on a sole trader's balance sheet will also be found on the balance sheet of a limited company.

1 Final accounts and balance sheet

In this topic you will learn:

- many terms and features of limited companies

- how to prepare the final accounts of a limited company, including a profit and loss appropriation account that records corporation tax, interim and final dividends, and transfers to general reserves

- how to prepare the balance sheet of a limited company that takes account of current liabilities such as corporation tax, final proposed dividends, debenture interest due, long-term liabilities including debentures, and details of shares and reserves.

Understanding limited companies: the fundamentals

Here is a summary of the main points you need to know. Throughout, there are examples to support your understanding. Please note that, for convenience, 'limited liability companies' are often referred to as 'limited companies'.

Who owns a limited company?

Limited liability companies are owned by **shareholders,** each of whom has an investment (shareholding) in the company. Shareholders are sometimes referred to as members of the company. Shareholders do not take part in the day-to-day running of a company unless they also happen to be **directors** of the company. Shareholders' involvement with the running of a company is normally limited to attending an **annual general meeting**. Since shares usually have voting rights, shareholders can vote for the election of individual directors at the annual general meeting (AGM).

Why 'limited liability'?

Limited liability in the title of a company means the company has limited liability for the debts of the business. Shareholders can lose their investment if the company fails but no more than that. Unlike a sole trader (or partner in a partnership) the private possessions of a shareholder cannot be used to settle the outstanding debts of a failing company. Strictly speaking shareholders have responsibility for the debts of the company to the extent they have invested, or agreed to invest, in the company.

Types of limited company

Limited companies are primarily of two types: private and public companies.

Private companies have the abbreviation 'Ltd' in their title. Those entitled to become shareholders in private companies are restricted to the individuals who established the company, their families and friends, and employees of the company. In other words, general members of the public cannot be shareholders and it is not possible to buy shares in a private limited company on a stock exchange. There must be at least one shareholder in a private limited company.

■ Illustration

Zextra Ltd an example of a private limited company

Zextra Ltd is a private limited company. The founders of the company, David and Sandra Ratcliffe, are the major shareholders having invested a considerable amount of money. However, some relations and friends have also invested in shares. All these shareholders are aware that they could lose the amount they have invested if the company is unsuccessful, but appreciate that this is the maximum they can lose.

Public companies have the abbreviation 'plc' in their title. As the title suggests, members of the public may invest in these companies. Shareholders often come from a wide range of investors including private individuals and 'institutional investors'. Institutional investors include other companies (for example, banks and insurance companies); some of the pension funds built up by other institutions may be invested in public limited companies. Public companies must have at least two shareholders and there is no limit on the maximum number of shareholders. Public companies tend to be very large scale organisations and they must have a share capital of at least £50,000 (there is no such requirement for a private limited company).

Shares and dividends

There are two (main) types of share: ordinary and preference. All shares are of a particular denomination. The usual face value (**par** or **nominal value**) of a share is £1, but some shares have a face value of 50p, £5, etc.

Ordinary shares (called **equity shares**) are the most common type of share. The owners of ordinary shares receive a dividend that varies depending on the amount of the company's profits. These are the owners who are the risk takers. Usually each ordinary share carries one vote. Ordinary shareholders, because they have votes, are able to control a limited company.

Preference shareholders receive a fixed dividend. The term '**preference shares**' is used for these shares because they rank before ordinary shareholders for the payment of dividends, i.e. are paid before ordinary shareholders. Because preference shareholders receive a fixed dividend, they are seen as taking less risk than ordinary shareholders who may do well or badly depending on how successful the company is. Normally preference shareholders do not have voting rights.

■ **Link**

For more information on limited companies, see Chapter 5, page 79.

■ **Case study**

'Zextra Ltd'

Zextra Ltd commenced trading on 1 January 2002. It has two directors, David Ratcliffe and his wife Sandra, who were responsible for establishing the company. The company specialises in providing high-quality organic soups made from the finest ingredients.

■ **Key terms**

Shareholders: the owners of a limited liability company.

Directors: are the senior managers of a limited company; they are appointed by shareholders at the AGM.

Annual general meeting: often called the AGM, is the yearly company meeting that can be attended by shareholders.

Private company: one in which only the founders of the company, their family, friends and employees can invest in shares.

Public company: one in which any member of the public can invest as shares are floated on the open market.

Ordinary shares: shares that carry voting rights and have a variable dividend that is dependent on the amount of profits.

Par value; nominal value: the face value of a share.

Equity shares: are ordinary shares.

Preference shares: shares that have a fixed rate of dividend and normally have no voting rights.

Key terms

Authorised capital: the maximum amount of capital the company can issue by way of shares.

Issued capital: the amount of shares that the company has chosen to issue to date.

In the event of a company failing (going into 'liquidation'), preference shareholders have a prior claim over ordinary shareholders in regard to the repayment of capital.

Shareholders received dividends when there are profits available for distribution. A company that has no profits or revenue reserves (see below) cannot pay any dividends.

Authorised and issued capital

Limited companies have an 'authorised' and 'issued' capital. **Authorised capital** is the maximum value of shares that the company can issue. Those who form the company decide this figure right at the outset, but they can increase the authorised capital at a later date if they so wish. The **issued capital** is the value of the shares that have already been issued; it will be equal to, or less than, the authorised capital.

Illustration

Using the basic terms associated with limited companies

Zextra Ltd has an authorised capital made up of 100,000 6% preference shares of £1 each and 900,000 ordinary shares of 50p each. The issued capital is made up of all the preference shares and 600,000 ordinary shares.

What this means is as follows:

The face value of the Zextra Ltd's shares is: £1 (preference shares); 50p (ordinary shares)

The total potential (authorised) capital of the company is £550,000 (Preference shares £100,000 + Ordinary shares £450,000).

The total issued capital is £400,000 (Preference Shares £100,000 + £300,000 Ordinary shares).

The preference shareholders are entitled to receive a fixed dividend of 6%. This would amount to £6,000 per annum (i.e. 6% × the issued preference share capital of £100,000).

The ordinary shareholders will receive a dividend based on the issued ordinary share capital of £300,000. The amount of the dividend will depend on the profits made by the company and the directors' decisions about how best to use the profits.

Activity

Stephen and Carole were the founder members of the private limited company called Beltramina Ltd. They planned that the company should have a maximum shareholding of 1m ordinary shares of £1 each and 200,000 7% preference shares of £1 each. Initially, shareholders were able to purchase 400,000 ordinary shares and 150,000 preference shares. State the following:

- the face value of the shares
- the amount of the company's authorised capital
- the amount of the company's issued capital
- the dividend that preference shares will hope to receive each year.

What happens to a company's profits?

A company's profits belong to its shareholders. At the end of a financial year the directors must decide how the profits should be used and shared out (appropriated). Some profits will be distributed as dividends, but others will be retained in the company. Retained profits are sometimes called **retained earnings**. For more about the appropriation of profits see below.

The directors of a limited company may decide to transfer some of the undistributed profits to a separate account. This account is called the '**general reserve**'. These profits can still be distributed as dividends, but, by making this transfer, the directors are indicating that it is the intention to retain the profits in the long term.

Retained earnings and the general reserve together form what are called the **revenue reserves** of a company.

The profits of limited companies are taxed. Companies pay **corporation tax** to the HM Revenue and Customs. (Note: sole traders and partnerships pay income tax on their profits.) Corporation tax becomes a current liability payable nine months after the end of the company's financial year.

Key terms

Retained earnings: undistributed profits arising from the normal course of business.

General reserve: part of the company's profits that has been set aside to indicate that it is likely to be retained within the company for the foreseeable future.

Revenue reserves: profits that arise from everyday trading activities and that can be distributed as dividends.

Corporation tax: tax on a company's profits.

Illustration

The directors of Zextra Ltd make decisions about the company's first year profits

Zextra Ltd made a profit of £160,000 during its first year of trading, i.e. for the year ended 31 December 2002. The company's accountant has explained to the two directors, David and Sandra Ratcliffe, that making a profit does not mean there is this amount of cash stored away in the company's bank account. The accountant has gone on to explain that much of the extra wealth that has been created as a result of making a profit is now tied up in trade debtors, stocks, additional fixed assets and so on. They are aware that part of the profits will be subject to corporation tax, which they must pay before 30 September 2003. They are also aware that they should pay a preference share dividend of £6,000 since there are sufficient profits available to do this. They have discussed what they should do about the remaining profits. They have debated how much profits should be used to finance an ordinary share dividend, conscious that their ordinary shareholders will expect some reward for investing in the company. They are aware that any dividend announcement will lead to a cash outflow in due course. They have carefully weighed up financing dividends with the need to retain some profits. They have decided it would be sensible to transfer some of the retained profits to a general reserve, to indicate to all the shareholders that these profits are unlikely to be used to finance dividends in the near future.

Preparing a company's final accounts

Illustration

Prepare Zextra Ltd's profit and loss and profit and loss appropriation accounts

The following summarised details have been extracted from the books of Zextra Ltd at the end of its second financial year, 31 December 2003.

	£
Auditors' fees	4,700
Business expenses	62,300
Depreciation of fixed assets	27,000
Directors' fees	58,000
Gross Profit	263,000
Issued capital	
100,000 6% preference shares of £1 each fully paid	100,000
600,000 ordinary shares of 50p each fully paid	300,000
Profit and loss account balance at 1 January 2003	44,600

Prepare the company's profit and loss and profit and loss appropriation account for the year ended 31 December 2003. The following additional information is available:

- provision should be made for corporation tax of £22,800
- the directors have decided to propose payment of the preference share dividend and a dividend of 5p per share on the ordinary shares
- the directors have decided to transfer £40,000 to a general reserve.

Some explanatory notes

Auditors' fees: all but the smallest limited companies are required to have their accounts audited. The auditors check the accounts to ensure they represent a true and fair view of the company's affairs. The auditors' fees (sometimes called auditors' remuneration) should be treated as an expense.

Directors' fees: these are amounts paid to the directors for the work they do in running the company (sometimes called directors' remuneration or directors' emoluments). Directors' fees should also be treated as an expense.

Profit and loss account balance: companies do not usually appropriate all their profits, so a balance remains on the profit and loss appropriation account (often called **retained earnings for the year**). The balance is carried forward to the next financial year. It can either be distributed in the next financial year, or be left undistributed. Usually the profit and loss account balance accumulates over time. It is shown on the company's balance sheet (more details below).

Profit after taxation: this label is used in a profit and loss appropriation account for the figure shown after corporation tax has been deducted from net profit for the year.

ZEXTRA LTD		
Profit and Loss Account for the year ended 31 December 2003		
	£	£
Gross profit		263,000
Less: business expenses	62,300	
auditors' fees	4,700	
directors' fees	58,000	
Depreciation of fixed assets	27,000	
		152,000
Net profit		111,000

Profit and Loss Appropriation Account for the year ended 31 December 2003		
	£	£
Net Profit		111,000
Less: Corporation tax		22,800
Profit after taxation		88,200
proposed final dividends		
preference shares	6,000	
ordinary shares	30,000	
transfer to general reserve	40,000	
		76,000
Retained earnings for the year		12,200

Figure 8.1 *Final accounts of limited companies*

Explanatory notes:

Preference share dividend: is 6% based on issued preference share capital £100,000, i.e. £6,000.

Ordinary share dividend: is 5p × the number of issued ordinary shares (i.e. 600,000 × 5p), i.e. £30,000.

Retained earnings: on 1 January the company already had retained earnings of £44,600 (the balance on the profit and loss account); by 31 December the retained earnings has increased to £56,800 (i.e. the original profit and loss balance £44,600 plus this year's undistributed profit £12,200). The updated figure for retained earnings will appear on the company's balance sheet.

Preparing a company's balance sheet

Illustration

Zextra Ltd's balance sheet at 31 December 2004

On 31 December 2004 the following balances remained in the books of Zextra Ltd <u>after</u> the preparation of the company's profit and loss and appropriation account for the year ended on that date.

	Dr	Cr
	£	£
Accruals		480
Cash at bank	10,980	
Corporation tax due		28,640
Fixed assets		
cost	620,000	
provision for depreciation		76,900
General reserve		65,000
Issued capital		
100,000 6% preference shares of £1 each fully paid		100,000

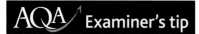
600,000 ordinary shares of 50p each fully paid		300,000
Prepayments	520	
Proposed dividends		
ordinary shares		45,000
preference shares		6,000
Retained earnings		23,800
Stock at 31 December 2004	19,700	
Trade creditors		14,880
Trade debtors	9,500	
	660,700	660,700

Figure 8.2 *Preparing a company's balance sheet*

Prepare the company's balance sheet at 31 December 2004.

Zextra Ltd			
Balance Sheet at 31 December 2004			
	£	£	£
FIXED ASSETS	Cost	Total Deprcn	Net
	620,000	76,900	543,100
CURRENT ASSETS			
Stock	19,700		
Trade debtors	9,500		
Prepayments	520		
Cash at bank	10,980		
		40,700	
Less CREDITORS: AMOUNTS FALLING DUE WITHIN ONE YEAR			
Trade creditors	14,880		
Accruals	480		
Corporation tax due	28,640		
Proposed dividends			
Ordinary shares	45,000		
Preference shares	6,000		
		95,000	
NET CURRENT LIABILITIES			(54,300)
			488,800
CAPITAL AND RESERVES			
Issued capital:			
600,000 ordinary shares of 50p each fully paid			300,000
100,000 6% preference shares of £1 each fully paid			100,000
General reserve			65,000

Retained earnings		23,800
		488,800
Authorised capital:		
100,000 6% preference shares of £1 each		
900,000 ordinary shares of 50p each		

Figure 8.3 *Company balance sheet*

Explanatory notes:

Creditors: amounts falling due within one year is a term currently used on company balance sheets as a subheading rather than the more familiar 'Current liabilities'.

Corporation tax and dividends on balance sheets: because both the corporation tax and proposed dividends will not have been paid at the time of the balance sheet they appear in the list of 'creditors: amounts falling due within one year'.

Net current liabilities: this term is used where, as in this example, there is negative working capital.

Capital and reserves: contrast this section with the capital section on a sole trader's balance sheet. There are similarities: the sole trader's investment (opening capital) is replaced by the shareholders' investment (issued shares) and the sole trader's net profit less drawings is replaced with reserves (i.e. profits not distributed to the shareholders). Issued shares have been described as 'fully paid'. This means that the shareholders have paid all the amounts due on the shares.

Understanding limited companies: additional matters

Here are some additional points that will help you develop an understanding of limited liability companies.

Debentures

Debentures are loans, and as such are part of the long-term liabilities of a company. It is important to avoid confusing debentures (liabilities) and ordinary and preference shares (capital). Debenture is technically the name of the document recording details of the loan.

Debentures carry a fixed rate of interest that is usually paid in two six-monthly instalments. Debenture interest is an ordinary expense of the company and is charged to the profit and loss account.

Debenture holders are paid ahead of shareholders in the event of a company failure. It is possible that the loan will be secured on a fixed asset of the company (example: freehold property). In this case the proceeds of the sale of the fixed asset are used to pay back the loan should the company go into liquidation, or to pay debenture interest if this has not been paid.

Debentures/loan stock should be shown under the heading **'Creditors: amounts falling due after more than one year'** on the company's balance sheet. This heading is the equivalent of 'long-term liabilities' that

> **Key terms**
>
> **Creditors: amounts falling due within one year:** a balance sheet subheading used for a company's current liabilities.
>
> **Debentures:** loans to a company on which a fixed rate of interest is paid. The interest is an expense to be charged to the profit and loss account.
>
> **Creditors: amounts falling due after more than one year:** a balance sheet subheading used for a company's long-term liabilities.

■ **Key terms**

Shareholders' funds: the total of issued capital and all reserves.

■ **Key terms**

Share premium: the amount paid for a share above its face value.

Capital reserve: profits that have been set aside and do not originate from the everyday trading activities of the company. Capital reserves cannot be distributed as dividends.

Interim dividend: a half-yearly dividend.

is used on a sole trader's balance sheet. Place this heading as the final item in the first part of the balance sheet (i.e. deduct from net assets).

Shareholders' funds

'**Shareholders' funds**' is a term used to describe the total issued capital and reserves.

■ **Activity**

Edan Ltd is partly financed by 8% debentures (repayable 2012) totalling £360,000 that were issued in 2004. During the year ended 31 December 2007 the company has paid debenture holders £14,400 in debenture interest.

a How much debenture interest should be recorded in the company's profit and loss account for the year ended 31 December 2007?

b How much debenture interest should be shown on the company's balance sheet at 31 December 2007?

c What information about debentures should be recorded under the heading (i) creditors: amounts falling due within one year; (ii) creditors: amounts falling due after more than one year?

Share premium

Once a company is established the value of its ordinary shares will vary. For example, if the original par (face) value of share was £1 its value will increase as the company builds up undistributed profits. If the company makes a fresh issue of shares it is permitted (by law) to offer these at a price in excess of the **par value or nominal value** of the shares. The extra amount is called the '**share premium**'.

The 'share premium' is a reserve. On a company's balance sheet it should be placed under the heading reserves and be the first in the list.

The share premium is known as a '**capital reserve**'. This technical term implies that the reserve did not arise from normal trading activities. The Companies Acts forbid capital reserves to be used to finance cash dividends for shareholders.

Interim dividends

The directors of a limited company can pay a dividend mid-year. These dividends are called **interim dividends**. If this happens preference shareholders will receive half of their fixed dividend, and ordinary shareholders will receive a dividend agreed by the directors. At the year-end all dividends, including interim dividends, must be shown in the appropriation account. However, because the interim dividends will already have been paid they will not appear as a current liability on the balance sheet.

 Activity

The directors of a limited company have agreed the payment of an interim dividend of 3p per share to the company's ordinary shareholders. Currently, the company has an issued ordinary share capital of £400,000 consisting of 50p ordinary shares.

a Calculate the total amount of the interim dividend to be paid to ordinary shareholders.

b Explain whether or not the interim dividend will appear on the company's balance sheet prepared at the end of the financial year.

Illustration

Zextra Ltd issues shares at a premium and debentures

The directors of Zextra Ltd decided that it was a good time for the company to expand. It was agreed that the 300,000 remaining ordinary shares should be issued. The face value of these shares was, of course, 50p each. However, the directors decided that because of the company's success they could be issued at 75p each. In addition, it was agreed that the company should borrow £50,000 by issuing 7% debentures redeemable in 2020.

The results of these decisions are as follows.

Shares: the issued share capital of the company will increase by 300,000 × 50p ordinary shares (i.e. £150,000).

Share premium: each ordinary share will raise an additional 25p because they are issued at 75p each, bringing in a total of 300,000 × 25p (i.e. £75,000).

The **total cash** raised by the share issue is £225,000.

Debentures: the debenture issue will raise cash £50,000. The loan will be shown as a separate long-term liability on the balance sheet.

Debenture interest: each year interest on the debentures must be paid; this will amount to 7% × £50,000, i.e. £3,500 per annum.

Activity

The directors of a limited company have proposed the issue of 60,000 ordinary shares with a face value of £1 at a price of £1.75 per share.

a   Calculate the amount of the share premium.

b   Calculate the total amount received from the share issue.

c   Should the share premium be included in a calculation of the shareholders' funds?

Preparing a company's final accounts and balance sheet

Illustration

Preparing Zextra final accounts and balance sheet including additional matters

Zextra Ltd's trading and profit and loss account for the year ended 31 December 2006 has already been prepared. The following information is available.

	Dr	Cr
	£	£
Accruals		200
Cash at bank	18,400	
7% Debentures (2020)		50,000
Fixed assets		
cost	960,000	
provision for depreciation		105,500
General reserve		74,000
Interim dividend: preference shares	3,000	
Interim dividend: ordinary shares	18,000	
Issued capital		
100,000 6% preference shares of £1 each fully paid		100,000
900,000 ordinary shares of 50p each fully paid		450,000
Net profit for the year		160,000

Prepayments	600	
Retained earnings at 1 January 2006		21,400
Share Premium		75,000
Stock in trade	27,300	
Trade creditors		8,900
Trade debtors	17,700	
	1,045,000	1,045,000

Figure 8.4 *Company's trial balance*

Additional information at 31 December 2006:

▪ Corporation tax due £25,000.

▪ The directors have decided to transfer £15,000 to reserves.

▪ The directors have proposed the payment of the second half of the preference share dividend, and a final dividend of 5p per share on the ordinary shares.

Prepare the company's profit and loss appropriation account for the year ended 31 December 2006 and a balance sheet as at that date.

Zextra Ltd Profit and Loss Appropriation Account for the year ended 31 December 2006		
	£	£
Net profit for the year		160,000
Less: Corporation tax		25,000
Profit after taxation		135,000
Less: interim dividends		
preference shares	3,000	
ordinary shares	18,000	
final proposed dividends		
preference shares	3,000	
ordinary shares	45,000	
transfer to general reserve	15,000	
		84,000
Retained earnings for the year		51,000

Balance Sheet at 31 December 2006			
	£	£	£
FIXED ASSETS	Cost	Total Deprcn	Net
	960,000	105,500	854,500
CURRENT ASSETS			
Stocks	27,300		
Trade debtors	17,700		
Prepayments	600		
Cash at bank	18,400		

		64,000	
less CREDITORS: AMOUNTS FALLING DUE WITHIN ONE YEAR			
Trade creditors	8,900		
Accruals	200		
Corporation tax due	25,000		
Proposed final dividends			
preference shares	3,000		
ordinary shares	45,000		
		82,100	
NET CURRENT LIABILITIES		(18,100)	
			836,400
CREDITORS: AMOUNTS FALLING DUE AFTER MORE THAN ONE YEAR			
7% Debentures (2020)			(50,000)
			786,400

CAPITAL AND RESERVES			
Issued shares			
900,000 ordinary shares of 50p each fully paid			450,000
100,000 6% preference shares of £1 each fully paid			100,000
Share premium			75,000
General reserve			89,000
Retained earnings			72,400
SHAREHOLDERS' FUNDS			786,400
Authorised capital:			
100,000 6% preference shares of £1 each			
900,000 ordinary shares of 50p each			

Figure 8.5 *Company's final accounts*

Calculations:

Final dividends: the final dividend on the preference shares is the other half of their fixed dividend, i.e. 6% × £100,000 × ½ = £3,000. The final dividend on the ordinary shares is 5p per share on 900,000 shares (i.e. 900,000 × 5p) which is £45,000.

Retained earnings: this is the total of retained earnings brought forward from the previous year (£21,400) and the balance remaining on this year's appropriation account (£51,000), i.e. £72,400.

Operating profit

You could be asked to calculate a limited company's **operating profit**. This figure is found by taking the net profit of the company and adding

> **Key terms**
>
> **Operating profit**: profit before interest charges and tax (i.e. net profit + interest).

back any interest charges. The figure is used in some accounting ratios (see Chapter 9) to assess the performance of the company. The usual definition of operating profit is that it is profit before interest and tax.

■ Illustration

Calculating operating profit

Zextra Ltd made a net profit of £160,000 during the year ended 31 December 2006. In order to find the company's operating profit for that financial period it would be necessary to add back any interest charges. Zextra Ltd has 7% debentures of £50,000.

So operating profit for the year ended 31 December 2006 would be: £160,000 add back debenture interest for year of £3,500 (i.e. 7% × £50,000), to give £163,500.

◧✔ *Learning outcomes*

As a result of studying this topic, you should now be able to:

- define a wide range of terms associated with limited companies

- prepare the trading and profit and loss account of a limited company including entries for debentures interest, directors' remuneration and auditors' fees

- prepare the profit and loss appropriation of a limited company including entries for corporation tax, interim and final dividends and transfers to general reserve and identifying the subtotal for profit after tax and the final balance of retained earnings for the year

- prepare the balance sheet of a limited liability company to include additional current liabilities (to be called creditors amounts falling due within one year) such as proposed dividends, corporation tax due, debenture interest due; long-term liabilities (to be called creditors amounts falling due after more than one year) including debentures and details of issued shares and reserves including share premium, general reserve and retained earnings

---

 Examination-style questions

✔ **1** Tentrix Ltd has an issued capital consisting of 200,000 8% preference shares of £1 each and 1 million ordinary shares of £1 each.

During the year ended 31 December 2007 the company made a net profit of £320,000.

The directors have made the following decisions:

1   to provide for corporation tax on the year's profits of £68,000

2   to propose the payment of the preference share dividend and a dividend of 15% on the ordinary shares

3   to transfer £50,000 to a general reserve.

Prepare the company's profit and loss appropriation account for the year ended 31 December 2007.

2   After the preparation of final accounts, the following balances remained in the books of Ardento Ltd.

	Dr £	Cr £
Accruals		750
Cash at bank	10,970	
Corporation tax due		27,880
Fixed assets		
cost	990,000	
provision for depreciation		148,500
General reserve		42,000
Issued capital		
50,000 7% preference shares of £1 each		
fully paid		50,000
650,000 ordinary shares of £1 each		
fully paid		650,000
Prepayments	480	
Proposed dividends		68,500
Retained earnings		23,280
Stock in trade	15,210	
Trade creditors		17,590
Trade debtors	11,840	
	1,028,500	1,028,500

Note: the company's authorised capital consists of 100,000 7% preference shares of £1 each and 800,000 ordinary shares of £1 each.

Prepare the company's balance sheet at 31 December 2007.

3   ACC3 June 2003

The draft profit for the year ended 31 May 2007 of Srian Ltd is £12,000,000. The following information for the year has not been taken into account.

	£
Ordinary dividends – paid	800,000
– proposed	1,300,000
Directors' fees	1,500,000
Provision for corporation tax	2,600,000
Debenture interest paid	1,200,000
Transfer to general reserve	1,000,000

Prepare the profit and loss appropriation account for the year ended 31 May 2007.

4   ACC3 January 2005

The following trial balance has been extracted from the books of Inthics Ltd after the preparation of the profit and loss account and the appropriation account.

Trial Balance at 31 December 2007		
	£	£
Issued ordinary shares of £1 each		240,000
Fixed assets at cost	900,000	

Provision for depreciation of fixed assets		320,000
Trade debtors	22,000	
Trade creditors		7,000
Accrued expenses		11,000
Prepaid expenses	8,000	
Bank balance		7,620
Provision for corporation tax		9,700
Proposed dividends		18,000
Share premium account		120,000
General reserve		60,000
Profit and loss account		174,680
Closing stock at 31 December 2007	38,000	
	968,000	968,000

Prepare a balance sheet at 31 December 2007.

5   ACC3 January 2004

Arthur wishes to purchase £1,000 worth of ordinary shares in Cerne Ltd, a new company. The company has an authorised ordinary share capital of 1,000,000 ordinary shares of £1 each. The company is to issue the shares at a price of £2.50 each.

Arthur says 'I would like to purchase the authorised shares because they are cheaper than the issued shares.'

Explain to Arthur the difference between the authorised ordinary share capital and the issued share capital of Cerne plc.

Explain to Arthur why the authorised shares have a nominal value of only £1 each and yet they are being issued at a price of £2.50 each.

6   ACC3 June 2002

The following information has been extracted from the books of account of Leroy McDade Ltd as at 31 December 2007.

	£
Issued share capital:	
Ordinary shares of 50p each fully paid	1,600,000
7% debentures (2020–2025)	200,000
Share premium account	800,000
Profit and loss account balance 1 January 2007	612,000
General reserve	150,000
Interim ordinary dividend paid 4 August 2007	40,000
Trade creditors	78,200
Directors' fees	117,000
Provision for corporation tax due	180,000

Additional information:

Net profit for the year after interest but before taxation was £546,000.

Debenture interest is payable half-yearly to 30 June and 31 December. It is paid to debenture holders on 27 July and 27 January each year.

The directors propose a transfer to general reserve of £50,000 and a final ordinary dividend of 5p per share.

Prepare the profit and loss appropriation account for the year ended 31 December 2007 of Leroy McDade plc.

Prepare balance sheet extracts at 31 December 2007 for Leroy McDade Ltd showing the sections for:

- the capital and reserves; and
- creditors falling due within one year (i.e. current liabilities).

7   ACC3 January 2001

Harriet Thing recently won some money on the national lottery. She wishes to invest £10,000 of her win in Tesdrales Ltd, a local company. She seeks your advice on whether to purchase:

- 80,000 7% preference shares of £1 each; or
- 40,000 ordinary shares of £1 each.

Harriet is rather puzzled to note that even though the amount to be invested in the shares of her choice would be the same, i.e. £10,000, fewer ordinary shares would be acquired.

Write a memorandum to Harriet:

(a)   explaining why an investment of £10,000 would give her only 8,000 preference shares or only 4,000 ordinary shares,

(b)   advising her, with reasons, which investment you consider would be better.

2 Final accounts and balance sheets: more advanced matters

In this topic you will learn:

- about revaluation of fixed assets
- to explain rights issue of shares
- to explain bonus issue of shares
- to prepare a company's balance sheet after a revaluation, rights and/or bonus issue.

Case study

Brix Ltd

Brix Ltd is a well-established company with an authorised capital of 6m ordinary shares of £1 each. On 1 January 2005 the company's issued capital consisted of 2m ordinary shares. Brix Ltd produces car radios and cd players that are sold to some of Europe's leading car manufacturers.

The revaluation of fixed assets

How does a revaluation of a fixed asset affect a company's balance sheet?

The directors of a company can revalue a fixed asset if they feel that its balance sheet value is significantly different from its market value. It is, of course, a common experience for individuals and businesses to find that freehold property, in particular, has increased in value over a period of years, sometimes quite substantially.

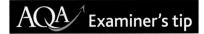

When a revaluation takes place the effect on balance sheet components is as follows:

Fixed asset: increased in value by the amount of the revaluation

Revaluation reserve: appears in the list of reserves at the amount of the revaluation

The double entry for a revaluation is:

Debit   Fixed asset

Credit   Revaluation reserve

The increase in value of the fixed asset is, of course, a gain for the company. However, this gain must not be shown in the company's profit and loss account, and it must not be used to 'finance' any cash dividends for shareholders. The law does not permit this because there is no cash to support the increase in the value. In other words, the revaluation reserve is, like the share premium, an example of a capital reserve.

Rights issues

What is a rights issue of shares?

This is an issue of shares by a company designed to raise cash, but it has some special features to get round some of the problems that can arise from making a share issue to the general public. These potential problems are as follows:

- there can be no guarantee that the shares will prove attractive to potential investors
- share issues are expensive because they can involve the use of specialist financial institutions to manage and administer the issue.

The directors of a company can try to get round these potential problems by offering the shares to existing shareholders. Each shareholder is offered additional shares in proportion to their existing shareholding. For example, a **rights issue** might be described as a "one for four" issue, meaning that a shareholder is offered one additional share for every four shares currently held. These shareholders have the right to take up the offer or to sell the rights to a third party – hence the term 'rights issue'. Offering shares to existing shareholders is less expensive than issues to the general public. Furthermore, right issues can be more successful than general issues. This is because the directors are likely to offer the shares at a special price, below the price that otherwise would have to be paid to acquire shares in the company.

There is an additional benefit of making a rights issue of shares: as the new shares are offered to existing shareholders, the control of the company remains with the same individuals as before.

How does a rights issue affect a company's balance sheet?

A rights issue affects a balance sheet in the same way as any other issue of shares for cash. The balance sheet items affected are as follows:

Bank: increases by the total cash proceeds from the share issue

Issued shares: increase by the face value of the shares issued

Share premium: increases by the additional amount raised by the share issue above the face value of the shares.

✓ Illustration

Revaluations and rights issues

The directors of Brix Ltd made the following decisions at 31 December 2006.

■ To revalue the freehold property by £700,000 to £2,500,000.

■ To make a rights issue of ordinary shares on 31 December 2006. Ordinary shareholders were offered 2 shares for every 5 shares currently held. The shares were offered at a price of £3.20 per share. The rights issue was fully subscribed.

Immediately before these decisions were implemented the company's trial balance was as follows:

	£000	£000
Freehold Property	1,800	
Other fixed assets	920	
Cash at bank	42	
Current assets (except bank)	254	
Current liabilities (creditors: amounts falling due within one year)		139
General reserve		280
Issued share capital:		
2m ordinary shares of £1 each		2,000
Retained earnings		317
Share premium		280
	3,016	3,016

Figure 8.6 *Company trial balance*

Brix Ltd

Balance Sheet as at 31 December 2006

	£000	£000	£000
Fixed assets			
Freehold Property at valuation		**2,500**	
Other fixed assets		920	
			3,420
Current assets	254		
Cash at bank	**2,602**		
		2,856	
less Creditors: amounts falling due within one year		139	
			2,717
			6,137
Capital and Reserves			
2.8 m ordinary shares of £1 each fully paid			**2,800**
Share premium			**2,040**
Revaluation reserve			**700**
General reserve			280
Retained earnings			317
			6,137

Figure 8.7 *Company balance sheet*

Activity

A company has an issued capital consisting of 900,000 ordinary shares of £1 each. The directors are now proposing they make a rights issue of shares and will offer existing ordinary shareholders 2 shares for every 3 currently held. The shares will be offered at a price of £2.70 per share. Assuming the rights issue is taken up by shareholders, calculate:

a   the cash received from the rights issue

b   the increase in the share premium arising from the rights issue.

Key terms

Bonus issue: the issue of additional shares to shareholders in proportion to their existing shareholders. No cash is paid for the additional shares. The issue is financed from the company's reserves, resulting in a re-structuring of the capital and reserves section of the balance sheet.

1   The effect of the revaluation is:

■ add £700,000 to freehold property so that it now appears at £2,500,000

■ include a revaluation reserve of £700,000 in the shares and reserves section of the balance sheet.

2   The rights issue will amount to 800,000 shares (i.e. 2 for 5 based on existing shareholding of 2 million shares).

3   The effect of the rights issue is:

■ increase bank balance by amount received: i.e. 800,000 × £3.20 = £2,560,000

■ increase the issued shares by the number of shares issued, i.e. 800,000 £1 shares (total value of issued shares now becomes £2,800,000)

■ increase the share premium by the amount of the premium charged on the shares issued, i.e. 800,000 × £2.20 = £1,760,000 (total value of share premium now becomes £2,040,000).

¹²₃ Bonus issues

What is a bonus issue?

A **bonus issue** of shares occurs when the directors of a company decide to change the structure of a company's balance sheet, increasing share capital at the same time as reducing reserves. Unlike a rights issue, there is no cash involved in a bonus issue. It is a technical alteration to the components in the 'share and reserves' section of the balance sheet. Bonus issues, sometimes called scrip issues, often occur where the issued capital and reserves become rather unbalanced, with share capital rather small compared to the reserves that have built up over the years, and not properly reflecting the value of the company's permanent assets. Shareholders receive additional shares, but do not make any payment for them. A 'one for two' bonus issue, for example, would mean that shareholders receive one additional share for every two shares currently held.

At first sight it sounds as if a bonus issue will be of considerable advantage to shareholders because they will own additional shares. However, the market price of the shares will adjust in proportion to the change in issued shares.

Illustration

Adjusting the market price of a share when a bonus issue takes place

Donald owned 100 £1 shares in a company. On 1 October 2007 the market price of the shares was £6 each. On 2 October 2007 the company made a bonus issue of one share for every two shares currently held. Donald looked forward to receiving an extra 50 shares, but noticed that the share price fell to £4 per share with the announcement of the bonus issue.

So Donald held 100 shares with a market price of £6 each on 1 October 2007, total value £600.

On 2 October 2007, Donald held 150 shares with a market price of £4 each, total value £600.

If the share price does not quite fall in proportion to the bonus issue, however, there will a financial advantage to shareholders, and this quite often happens. Shareholders may also gain for the following reasons.

- The shares become more marketable after a bonus issue, because the reduced market price makes the shares seem more attractive to potential investors.
- If the directors of the company maintain the usual rate of dividend, then shareholders will gain because they will receive dividends on the bonus shares as well as their original shareholding.

How does a bonus issue affect a balance sheet?

A bonus issue only affects the capital and reserves section of the balance sheet as follows:

Issued shares: increase by the value of the bonus shares

Reserves: reduce by the value of the bonus issue

Any reserve can be used to 'finance' a bonus issue. Often the opportunity is taken to use capital reserves, such as the share premium or revaluation reserve. If capital reserves are used rather than **revenue reserves**, the directors can be said to be 'maximising flexibility in regard to the payment of cash dividends', since only revenue reserves can be used to finance cash dividends.

Illustration

The effect of a bonus issue on a balance sheet

On 31 December 2007 the trial balance of Brix Ltd was as follows:

Balance Sheet at 31 December 2007 (before bonus issue)		
	£000	£000
Fixed assets		5,970
Current assets	250	
less Creditors: amounts falling due within one year	190	
		60
		6,030
Capital and reserves		
Ordinary shares: 2.8 m shares of £1 each		2,800
Share premium		2,040
Revaluation reserve		700
General reserve		350
Retained earnings		140
		6,030

Figure 8.8 *Company balance sheet*

On 31 December 2007 the directors decided to make a 1 for 1 bonus issue. The directors decided to maintain maximum flexibility in regard to the financing of cash dividends.

Balance Sheet at 31 December 2007 (**after bonus issue**)		
	£000	£000
Fixed assets		5,970
Current assets	250	
less Creditors: amounts falling due within one year	190	
		60
		6,030
Capital and reserves		
Ordinary shares: 5.6 m shares of £1 each		**5,600**
General reserve		**290**
Retained earnings		140
		6,030

Figure 8.9 *Company balance sheet*

Explanatory notes:

1 The bonus issues gives shareholders one extra share for each share already owned, so 2.8m shares will be issued (face value £1 each).
2 The value of the bonus issue is £2.8m.
3 The bonus issued will be financed from reserves: share premium £2,040,000 plus revaluation reserve £700,000 plus £60,000 from general reserve to total £2.8m.
4 The capital reserves are used first because the directors wish to maintain cash dividend flexibility.

Activity

The directors of each of the three companies listed below have decided to make a bonus issue of shares. In each case calculate the number of bonus shares that will be issued.

Company	Current issued capital	Face value of shares	Scale of bonus issue (number of bonus shares to number of existing shares)	Number of bonus shares
X Ltd	£3m	£1	1 for 2	
Y Ltd	£2.8m	50p	2 for 1	
Z Ltd	£1.5m	£5	3 or 4	

Table 8.1 *Bonus shares*

◊✔ *Learning outcomes*

As a result of studying this topic, you should now be able to:

- define revaluation of fixed assets, rights issues of shares and bonus issues of shares

- prepare a balance sheet to show the effects of a revaluation of fixed assets, a rights issues of shares and a bonus issue of shares

- evaluate rights issues by assessing the benefits and drawbacks of a rights issue of shares from the issuing company's viewpoint

- evaluate bonus issues by assessing the benefits and drawbacks of a bonus issue from the issuing company's viewpoint and from a shareholder's viewpoint

 Examination-style questions

✔ **1** Rentra Ltd's summarised balance sheet at 30 June 2007 was as follows:

	£000	£000
Fixed assets		
Freehold Premises	780	
Other fixed assets at net book value	450	
		1,230
Current assets	360	
less creditors: amounts falling due within one year	250	
		110
		1,340
Creditors: amounts falling due after more than one year		
8% Debentures		(400)
		940
Capital and reserves		
Ordinary shares: 1m of £1 each		400
Share premium		200
General reserve		190
Retained earnings		150
		940

The directors have decided to revalue the company's freehold property at £1,000,000 with immediate effect.

Prepare a new balance sheet immediately after the revaluation of the freehold property.

2   The directors of Ceffra Ltd have decided to make a rights issue of shares. The company's balance sheet immediately prior to the rights issue was as follows.

Balance Sheet at 30 September 2007

	£000	£000
Fixed assets at net book value		2,350
Current assets	428	
less Creditors: amounts falling due within one year	311	
		117
		2,467
Capital and reserves		
Ordinary shares: 1.6m shares of £1 each fully paid		1,600
Share premium		500
General reserve		228
Retained earnings		139
		2,467

The rights issue is of 1.2 m shares of £1 each offered at a premium of £1.40 each.

Prepare the company's balance sheet immediately after the rights issue. Assume the rights issue was fully subscribed.

3   The directors of Heldren Ltd have decided to make a bonus issue of shares. The company's balance sheet immediately before the bonus issue was as follows.

Balance Sheet at 31 March 2007

	£000
Fixed assets at net book value	6,850
Net current assets	736
	7,586
Creditors: amounts falling due after more than one year	
7% Debentures	(800)
	6,786
Capital and reserves	
Ordinary shares: 2m of £1 each	2,000
Share premium	1,500
Revaluation reserve	1,380
General reserve	1,133
Retained earnings	773
	6,786

Ordinary shareholders will be given 3 shares for every 2 shares currently held. The directors' policy is to maintain maximum flexibility in regard to the payment of cash dividends.

Prepare the company's balance sheet at 31 March 2007 immediately after the bonus issue.

4   The directors of Wimdron Ltd have decided to revalue the company's freehold property and to make a bonus issue of shares. Immediately prior to these events the company's balance sheet was as follows.

Balance Sheet at 31 August 2007

	£000	£000
Fixed assets		
Freehold property	1,450	
Other fixed assets at net book value	740	
		2,190
Net current assets		392
		2,582
CAPITAL AND RESERVES		
Ordinary shares: 2.4 m shares of 50p each fully paid		1,200
Share premium		720
General reserve		437
Retained earnings		225
		2,582

The freehold property is to be revalued at £2,000,000 on 1 September 2007. The revaluation will be followed on the same day by a bonus issue of shares of 5 shares for every 6 shares currently held. The directors have stated that in regard to financing the bonus issue, they wish to retain maximum flexibility in regard to the payment of cash dividends.

Prepare the company's balance sheet at 1 September 2007 following the revaluation and bonus share issue.

5   ACC6 June 2008

Frith Ltd made a bonus issue on 31 May 2007. The shares were issued on the basis of 1 share for every 4 held. The directors of the company wish to retain the reserves in their most distributable form.

The capital and reserves extract from the balance sheet *before* the issue is shown below.

Capital and reserves	£000
Ordinary shares of 10p each	1,600
Share premium account	250
Revaluation reserve	140
Profit and loss account	240
	2,230

Required

(a)   Prepare the capital and reserves extract from the balance sheet *after* the bonus issue.

(b)   Explain why a company might choose to make a bonus issue of shares.

(c)   Assess the effect of the bonus issue on an ordinary shareholder.

When assets are revalued, any surplus is transferred to a revaluation reserve rather than credited to the profit and loss account.

d   Explain, with reference to accounting concepts, why this is so.

Ratio analysis and the assessment of business performance

As you know, much hard work goes into preparing financial accounting records! All this effort would be largely wasted, however, if it was not used by interested parties, particularly owners and managers, to uncover how well or badly a business is performing. In this chapter you will learn some techniques for analysing business performance and learn how to judge just how well a business is doing. You will also be able to draw upon all your developing understanding of businesses to be able to suggest what should happen to further improve a business's performance. You will find that your skills in preparing final accounts and balance sheets of sole traders and limited companies will now be of considerable value in understanding what these statements show about a business's financial health. You will principally be looking at a business's profitability and liquidity, but you will also consider how a company arranges its finance and why this could matter to the company and its shareholders. You will learn not only how to calculate 11 ratios, and gain an appreciation of why ratio analysis is useful but also why this process has its limitations. You will be learning how to write effective reports on business performance, in which you provide a careful evaluation of the business's financial strengths and weaknesses, based on ratio calculations and comparisons of the results with previous years or with other similar businesses.

1 Accounting ratios

In this topic you will learn:

- the names of, and formulae for, different ratios

- how to calculate each of the ratios

- how to explain why ratios are important

- how to explain the limitations of ratios

- how to explain the differences between cash and profit.

Case studies

'Bayford Stores' and 'Wexfield plc'

'Bayford Stores' is located in the centre of Bayford. The business is owned by Indira Khan and it sells electrical goods. The business has been trading for a number of years.

'Wexfield plc' is a national chain of high-quality hotels. The company is financed by a mix of preference shares, ordinary shares and debentures.

The value of ratios

Why are ratios used to assess business performance?

Ratios provide a means of comparing the performance of a business

- from one year to the next
- with other similar businesses

They enable changes in important aspects of a business's performance to be pinpointed and quantified. The calculation of ratios enables trends to be highlighted.

The owners and managers of businesses will be eager to use ratios to assess performance. Other **stakeholders** will also be keen to assess performance and rivals will be interested, too. In the case of limited companies, potential investors will also take an interest.

Limitations of ratios

Are there any limitations to the use of ratios when measuring business performance?

Ratio analysis is of limited value because:

- it is applied to recent financial performance, in other words it is based on historical data, which may or may not have any direct relevance as to how the business will perform in the future
- it tends to used summarised accounting information (as shown in final accounts and balance sheets) and this information may hide a more complex story of partial successes offset by partial failures
- it can only be used with financial information, and so it cannot be used to assess other important factors about a business such as the qualities of the management team, the morale of employees, etc.
- balance sheets are for a particular moment in time and may not be entirely representative of how the business usually performs
- it relies on making comparisons of similar businesses, yet, however similar businesses may appear, there are bound to be important factors that make them different (for example the owner's or directors' mission for the business; differing accounting policies in regard to, say, provisions for doubtful debts)
- it uses elements in financial accounts that may distort the picture (for example, the figure capital employed relies on totally the balance sheet values of assets, yet some of these – particularly property – may be undervalued on the balance sheet)
- it cannot be used effectively for comparisons of businesses that are totally different in nature
- it relies on interpreting results and that is bound to be a subjective process.

Trading account ratios

Which ratios are used to analyse a trading account and how are they calculated?

The three ratios used to analyse a trading account are as follows:

Gross profit margin	Gross Profit / Turnover x 100
Mark-up	Gross Profit / Cost of sales x 100
Rate of stock turnover	Cost of sales / Average stock

Key terms

Gross profit margin: gross profit in relation to turnover (measured as a percentage).

Mark-up: gross profit in relation to cost of sales (measured as a percentage).

Rate of stock turnover: cost of sales dividend by average stock.

Illustration

Calculating Bayford Stores's Trading Account Ratios

BAYFORD STORES
Trading Account for the year ended 31 December 2007

	£	£
Sales		360,000
Less: Opening stock	16,200	
Purchases	239,600	
	255,800	
Closing stock	15,800	
		240,000
Gross profit		120,000

Figure 9.1 *Trading account*

Gross profit margin

$$\frac{\text{Gross Profit}}{\text{Turnover}} \times 100 \quad \text{i.e.} \quad \frac{£120,000}{£360,000} \times 100 \quad \text{i.e.} \quad 33.33\%$$

Mark-up

$$\frac{\text{Gross Profit}}{\text{Cost of sales}} \times 100 \quad \text{i.e.} \quad \frac{£120,000}{£240,000} \times 100 \quad \text{i.e.} \quad 50\%$$

Rate of stock turnover

$$\frac{\text{Cost of sales}}{\text{Average stock}} \quad \text{i.e.} \quad \frac{£240,000}{£16,000*} \quad \text{i.e.} \quad 15 \text{ times}$$

* Average stock was found by taking the average of the opening stock (£6,200) and closing stock (£5,800)

$$\text{i.e.} \quad \frac{£6,200 + £5,800}{2} = £6,000$$

Background knowledge

It is possible to work out the rate of stock turnover in terms of days. In the example, average stock was sold 15 times during the year. This would be the equivalent of of a rate of stock turnover of 24 days (i.e. 365/15 days).

Background knowledge

The rate of stock turnover is given as 'so many times' – i.e. in the example the average stock was sold 15 times during the year. The formula to use if you wish to calculate the rate of stock turnover in days is:

$$\frac{\text{Average stock}}{\text{Cost of sales}} \times 365$$

Using the data in the example, the result would be 24 days. If both the opening and closing stocks are not available in the information provided, it is possible to use just the closing stock in calculations rather than an average stock figure.

☑ Profit and loss account ratios

Which ratios are used to analyse a profit and loss account and how are they calculated?

The two ratios used to analyse a profit and loss account are as follows:

Net profit margin	$\frac{\text{Net Profit}}{\text{Turnover}} \times 100$
Overhead to turnover	$\frac{\text{Overhead}}{\text{Turnover}} \times 100$

Illustration

Calculating Bayford Stores's Profit and Loss Account Ratios

BAYFORD STORES
Profit and Loss Account for the year ended 31 December 2007

	£	£
Gross Profit		120,000
Less: administration expenses	12,000	
rent, rates and insurance	18,000	
wages and salaries	48,000	
depreciation of fixed assets	18,000	
		96,000
Net Profit		24,000

Figure 9.2 *Profit and loss account*

Net profit margin

$\frac{\text{Net Profit}}{\text{Turnover}} \times 100$ i.e. $\frac{£24,000}{£360,000} \times 100$ i.e.   6.67%

Overhead/turnover

$\frac{\text{Administration expenses}}{\text{Turnover}} \times 100$ i.e. $\frac{£12,000}{£360,000} \times 100$ i.e.   3.33%

$\frac{\text{Rent, rates and insurance}}{\text{Turnover}} \times 100$ i.e. $\frac{£18,000}{£360,000} \times 100$ i.e.   5%

$\frac{\text{Wages and salaries}}{\text{Turnover}} \times 100$ i.e. $\frac{£48,000}{£360,000} \times 100$ i.e.   13.33%

$\frac{\text{Depreciation}}{\text{Turnover}} \times 100$ i.e. $\frac{£18,000}{£360,000} \times 100$ i.e.   5%

💡 Balance sheet ratios

Which ratios are used to analyse a balance sheet and how are they calculated?

The six ratios used to analyse a balance sheet are as follows:

Return on capital employed	*For a sole trader:*
	$\dfrac{\text{Net Profit}}{\text{Capital}} \times 100$
	Note: normally the opening capital is used for this ratio, but if this is not available it is possible to use the closing capital figure.
	For a limited company:
	$\dfrac{\text{Profit before interest and tax}}{\textbf{Capital employed}} \times 100$
Net current assets ratio (current ratio or working capital ratio)	Current assets: current liabilities
Liquid capital ratio (acid test ratio)	**Liquid capital**: current liabilities (liquid capital is current assets excluding stock)
Debtor collection period (in days)	$\dfrac{\text{Trade debtors}}{\text{Credit sales}} \times 365$
Creditor payment period (in days)	$\dfrac{\text{Trade creditors}}{\text{Credit purchases}} \times 365$
Gearing	$\dfrac{\text{Fixed return financing}}{\text{All sources of finance}} \times 100$ *For a limited company:* $\dfrac{\text{Preference shares + Long-term liabilities (e.g. debentures)}}{\text{Preference and Ordinary Shares + Reserves + Long-term liabilities}} \times 100$

Table 9.1 *Six ratios used to analyse a balance sheet*

 Activity

Sahera Ltd had a turnover of £20m in 2007. The company's gross profit for 2007 was £4.8 m; running costs for 2007 totalled £3.8 m. Calculate:

a the business's net profit

b the percentage net profit margin.

Activity

Ahmed & Co's turnover for a year was £1.5m and the business's cost of sales was £0.75m. Calculate

a the gross profit and then state

b the percentage mark-up and

c the percentage gross profit margin.

Key terms

Capital employed: for a limited company this is made up of shares + reserves + long-term liabilities.

Key terms

Return on capital employed: net profit in relation to capital invested (sole trader) or capital employed (limited company), expressed as a percentage. This is an important measure of profitability.

Net current assets ratio: is current assets in relation to current liabilities; the ratio is sometimes called the current ratio or the working capital ratio. This is an important measure of liquidity.

Liquid capital: is current assets excluding stock.

■ Activity

Kyle & Co's opening stock on 1 January 2007 was £88,000; on 31 December the closing stock was £72,000. During 2007 the business sold goods costing £960,000. Calculate:

a   the average stock for 2007

b   the rate of stock turnover for 2007 expressing your answer in days.

Background knowledge

Alternative formulas: there are a number of acceptable ways of measuring some ratios. For example, it is possible to use a sole trader's opening capital, closing capital, or an average of these when calculating a sole trader's return on capital invested. In the illustrations that follow, the opening capital has been used. There are a number of ways of measuring gearing. Again, any conventional formula would be accepted, but it is recommended that you use the formula given here.

Alternative names: some ratios have alternative names; any of the alternative names given here are accepted.

Illustration

Calculating Wexfield plc's balance sheet ratios

WEXFIELD plc
Balance Sheet at 31 December 2007

	£	£	£
Fixed assets at net book value			1,530
Current assets			
Stocks	217		
Trade debtors	114		
Prepayments	5		
Cash at bank	44		
		380	
less creditors: amounts falling due within one year			
Trade creditors	69		
Accruals	3		
Dividends	66		
Corporation tax	72		
		210	
			170
			1,700
Creditors: amounts falling due after more than one year 8% Debentures (2022)			(300)
			1,400
Capital and reserves			
1,600,000 ordinary shares of 50p each fully paid			800
200,000 7% preference shares of £1 each fully paid			200
Share premium			250
Retained earnings			150
			1,400

Figure 9.3 *Balance sheet*

Notes:

The company made a net profit of £210,000.

The company's total credit sales for the year ended 31 December 2007 were £1,400,000; credit purchases for the same period were £930,000.

Return on capital employed

$$\frac{\text{Net Profit before tax and interest}}{\text{Capital employed}} \times 100 \quad \text{i.e.} \quad \frac{£234,000}{£1,400,000} \times 100$$

i.e.   16.71%

Net profit before interest is calculated as follows: net profit £210,000 add back interest on debentures (8% x £300,000) = £210,000 + £24,000

Net current asset ratio/Current ratio/Working capital ratio

Current assets: current liabilities   i.e. £380,000: £210,000 i.e. 1.81:1

Liquid capital ratio/Acid test ratio

Liquid assets: current liabilities   i.e. £163,000: £210,000 i.e. 0.78:1

Debtor collection period

$$\frac{\text{Closing debtors}}{\text{Credit sales}} \times 365 \qquad \text{i.e.} \quad \frac{£114,000}{£1,400,000} \times 365 \quad \text{i.e. 29.72 days}$$

Creditor payment period

$$\frac{\text{Closing creditors}}{\text{Credit purchases}} \times 365 \qquad \text{i.e.} \quad \frac{£69,000}{£930,000} \times 365 \quad \text{i.e. 27.08 days}$$

Gearing

$$\frac{\text{Fixed return finance}}{\text{All sources of finance}} \times 100 \qquad \text{i.e.} \quad \frac{£500,000}{£1,700,000} \times 100 \quad \text{i.e. 29.41\%}$$

Fixed return finance is: preference share capital + debentures, i.e. £200,000 + £300,000, i.e. £500,000

All finance is: preference shares £200,000 + ordinary shares £800,000 + reserves £400,000 + debentures £300,000, i.e. £1,700,000

AQA Examiner's tip

Always state the formula you are using.

Background knowledge

The net current assets ratio and liquid capital ratio should always be expressed as xx: 1.

Background knowledge

The liquid capital (acid test) ratio excludes stock, this is because it is assumed that this is the least liquid of a business's current assets, i.e. takes the longest time to be turned into cash.

Activity

Ortega & Co had total current assets of £140,000 including a stock of £55,000, and current liabilities of £105,000 at 31 December 2007. Calculate:

a net current assets

b liquid assets

c net current assets ratio

d liquid capital ratio.

Activity

Phil Wentworth's business had credit sales totalling £328,500 during its most recently completed financial year. At the year-end trade debtors totalled £27,000. Calculate the debtor collection period in days.

Activity

Sarah Ratcliffe Ltd is financed by debentures £500,000 and shareholders' funds of £1,500,000. The company does not have any preference shares. Calculate the company's gearing ratio.

Cash versus profit

What are the differences between cash and profit?

Profits and cash are not necessarily the same for the following reasons.

Some accounting entries have an effect on profits but no effect on cash:

- depreciation of fixed assets
- provisions for doubtful debts

Some accounting entries have an effect on cash but no effect on the calculation of net profit:

- purchasing fixed assets
- borrowing money (including debentures in the case of a limited company)
- repaying loans (including debentures in the case of a limited company)
- owner's drawings (or dividends in the case of limited companies)
- additional capital introduced by the owner (or the issue of shares in the case of limited companies)
- payment of tax

Activity

Croxley Wholesale Ltd recently made annual profits of £400,000 but completed the year with a bank overdraft of £30,000. Identify **four** different types of transaction that might account for this situation.

Background knowledge

Sometimes the owners or managers of a business may think that, because their business has made a profit, there should be a substantial cash balance at the year end and may be puzzled if the bank balance is an overdraft. The reverse can also apply: a business can be operating at a loss yet have a satisfactory bank balance.

Some other transactions have an immediate effect on profits but a delayed effect on cash:

▓ credit sales

▓ credit purchases

▓ expense accruals

Some other transactions have an immediate effect on cash but a delayed effect on profit:

▓ unsold stock

▓ prepayments

▓ purchase of a fixed asset (leading to depreciation of the fixed asset)

💡✔ *Learning outcomes*

As a result of studying this topic, you should now be able to:

■ identify, state the formula for, and calculate the following ratios: gross profit margin, mark up, rate of stock turnover, net profit margin, expense to turnover, return on capital employed, net current assets (working capital) ratio, liquid capital (acid test) ratio, debtor collection period, creditor payment period, gearing

■ explain why ratios are important

■ explain the limitations of ratios

■ explain the differences between cash and profit

 Examination-style questions

✔ 1 Cheryl Adams, a retailer, presented the following final accounts for her business at the end of its most recently completed financial year.

Trading and Profit and Loss Account for the year ended 30 September 2007		
	£	£
Sales		720,000
Less Opening stock	49,000	
Purchases	532,000	
	581,000	
Closing stock	41,000	
Cost of sales		540,000
Gross profit		180,000
Less General expenses	18,000	
Rates and insurance	24,000	
Wages and salaries	72,000	
Depreciation of fixed assets	6,000	
		120,000
Net profit		60,000

Rate of stock turnover

What does the rate of stock turnover tell you about a business's performance?

The rate of stock turnover:

- compares the average stock to the total cost of stock sold during a period
- it indicates how quickly stocks are being sold.

If the rate is increasing:

- perhaps the business is selling more stock
- or perhaps the average stock held is being reduced.

If the rate is decreasing:

- perhaps the business is selling less stock
- or perhaps the business is holding more average stock.

For a business to see the rate of stock turnover increasing because it is selling more goods would, of itself, be an encouraging sign. The more sales the more chance to earn a gross profit. However, one would need to bear in mind why more stocks were being sold before making a final judgment. Perhaps there has been increased sales because of price cuts, for example, but if the price cut was too severe there could be a negative impact on gross profit.

For a business to see a change in the rate of stock turnover because average stock is changing could be interpreted in a variety of ways. To reduce average stocks could be a good move because the business could reduce its storage costs. On the other hand, if it goes too far with this, the choice available to customers may be reduced and this could impact on sales.

Further means of interpreting this ratio

If you know the typical rate of stock turnover for a type of business you can comment on whether a business's result is higher or lower and suggest why this might be happening. For example, if the rate of stock turnover is too low, you could suggest that possibly the business is charging too much for the goods it sells, which is depressing sales, or that it is holding too much average stock.

Net profit margin and overheads/turnover ratios

What does the net profit margin and overheads/turnover percentages tell you about a business's performance?

The **net profit margin** percentage tells you:

- how much net profit is being made in relation to sales
- how much net profit (in pence) is being made for every £1 of sales.

If the percentage is increasing, this tells you that:

- either the business is making more gross profit
- or that costs have been held at previous level or reduced
- or some combination of these factors.

If the percentage is decreasing, this tells you that:

- either the business is making less gross profit
- or that costs have risen above previous levels
- or some combination of these factors.

AQA Examiner's tip

Approach data in a simple way to start with, for example:

- what's happened to turnover (all businesses like to see this increasing as it is often the key to success)
- what has happened to the ratios: are they increasing or decreasing, or is the picture more mixed?
- is the pattern of change in the ratios a good thing or a bad thing for the business?

Then try to see if you can deduce any important information from the data that can help you make a judgement about the business's success. For example, in the illustration it is possible to work out that gross profit has been improving over the three-year period.

Then try to explain what may have caused the changes in the ratio.

Finally, have a clear view as to whether the business's performance is improving or not.

Background knowledge

The average figures for a type of business are sometimes called 'benchmarking data', 'industrial averages' or 'sector averages'.

The **overheads/turnover** percentage tells you:

■ how much is being spent on an overhead in relation to turnover

■ for each £1 of sales how much (in pence) is being paid for an overhead.

If the percentage is increasing, this tells you that:

■ the business is less efficient than it was previously in regard to controlling costs.

If the percentage is decreasing, this tells you that:

■ the business is more efficient than it was previously in regard to controlling costs.

Further means of interpreting these ratios

If you know the benchmark figures for a type of business, you can comment on whether the business is operating more efficiently or less efficiently than is usual.

Activity

Desdra Stores has improved its gross profit margin for its most recently completed financial year, but it has not made any changes to its pricing policy. At the same time, the rate of stock turnover has fallen. Furthermore, the net profit margin has declined. Identify one reason for:

a the improvement in the gross profit margin

b the fall in the rate of stock turnover

c the decline in the net profit margin.

Return on capital employed

What does the return on capital employed percentage tell you about a business's performance?

The **return on capital employed** percentage measures:

■ net profit in relation to capital employed

■ how much profit (in pence) is made for every £1 of capital employed.

If the return on capital employed percentage is increasing it tells you:

■ either the business is making more net profit

■ or the business has employed less capital

■ or some combination of both these factors

■ that the business is using its resources (in the form of assets) more effectively.

If the return on capital employed percentage is decreasing it tells you:

■ either the business is making less net profit

■ or the business has employed more capital

■ or some combination of both these factors

■ that the business is using its resources less effectively.

Further means of interpreting these ratios

A business's return on capital employed could be compared to the return for similar businesses if these benchmark figures are available. In the case of a sole trader, if might be possible to consider how well the sole trader would do if the capital tied up in the business were invested, and if the sole trader, instead, was in employment earning a salary. In making such a comparison, it would be important to remember how relatively risky it is to invest in a business compared to investing in a savings account.

Net current assets and liquid capital ratios

What do the net current assets and liquid capital ratios tell you about a business's performance?

The **net current assets ratio** measures:

- current assets in relation to current liabilities
- the amount of current assets available to pay the short-term 'debts' of the business.

The **liquid capital ratio** is similar because it measures:

- liquid assets in relation to current liabilities
- the amount of liquid assets available to pay 'the debts' of the business.

The difference between the ratios is one of timing. Net current assets looks at liquidity and cash flow issues further ahead than liquid capital. Liquid capital is a more immediate measure of liquidity (hence the term 'acid test ratio').

If the two ratios are *increasing:*

- this could imply that the business will find it easier to pay its debts (a strength)
- or that it has too many resources tied up as current assets or liquid capital (a weakness).

If the two ratios are *decreasing:*

- this could imply that the business will find it more difficult to pay its debts (a weakness)
- or that it has reduced the resources tied up as current assets or liquid capital to a more efficient level (a strength).

Whether the change in the ratios should be interpreted as a strength or a weakness depends on the benchmark figures for the type of business concerned. These benchmarks vary considerably. For example, a supermarket chain needs relatively low ratios in order to operate effectively, because their sales are overwhelmingly in cash and they tend to have a high rate of stock turnover for most of their products. Contrast this with, say, a furniture store, where there is likely to be a relatively high level of credit sales and relatively low rates of stock turnover.

> ## Activity
>
> Orbell Ltd's net profit has decreased considerably since last year, but its return on capital employed has improved. At the same time the business's liquid capital ratio has increased. Explain one reason why
>
> a the return on capital employed has improved
> b the liquid capital ratio has increased
> c the increase in the liquid capital ratio may be bad news for the business.

> ## Background knowledge
>
> Short-term 'debts' of the business would include all the items on which the business will need to use cash resources in the near future. These should include the current liabilities, such as trade creditors, but may also include:
>
> - many expenses (because these tend to be paid at frequent intervals)
> - loan repayments
> - the owner's drawings (or dividend payments for a limited company)
> - planned purchases of fixed assets
> - payments of tax.

> ## AQA Examiner's tip
>
> Avoid generalising about the correct net current assets ratio or liquid capital ratio for businesses to have. Some candidates write about an ideal ratio. This is to be avoided, because the appropriate ratio depends very much on the type of business. For example, compare supermarkets and furniture stores as illustrated in the main text.

■ Debtor collection period and creditor payment period

What does the debtor collection period and creditor payment period tell you about a business's performance?

The **debtor collection period** measures:

■ how many days on average a credit customer takes to pay.

If the debtor collection period is *increasing* this tells you that debtors are taking longer to pay than previously.

This change can be interpreted as being:

■ a weakness because it could imply that credit control is not being as carefully managed as previously and this could lead to an increase in bad debts

■ a strength if previously credit control was too tight, and the change has resulted in a greater volume of credit sales.

If the debtor collection period is *decreasing* this tells you that debtors are taking a shorter time to pay than previously.

This change can be interpreted as being:

■ a strength because it could imply that credit control is being more carefully managed than previously and this could reduce the amount of bad debts

■ a weakness if previously credit control was about right, and the change has resulted in a decline in credit sales because rival businesses offer better credit terms.

The **creditor payment period** measures:

■ how many days are taken on average to pay for credit purchases.

If the creditor payment period is *increasing* this tells you that a business is taking longer to pay its creditors than previously.

This change can be interpreted as being:

■ a weakness because it could mean that the business is exceeding the credit period allowed by suppliers and as a result suppliers may discontinue offering credit facilities

■ a strength as cash flow will be improved.

If the creditor payment period is *decreasing* this tells you that the business is taking less time to pay creditors.

This change can be interpreted as being:

■ a strength because it could imply that credit control is being more carefully managed and that difficulties with suppliers over exceeding credit limits will no longer occur

■ a weakness if the business is now paying suppliers earlier than necessary, resulting in a negative impact on cash flow.

Further means of interpreting these ratios

It is useful to compare the debtor collection period with the creditor payment period. If the creditor payment period is shorter than the debtor collection period this will have a negative impact on cash flow. If the situation is reversed, i.e. debtors pay more quickly than the business pays suppliers, this will have a positive impact on cash flow. The latter is recommended for long-term cash management control.

✓ Illustration

Assessing the performance of Bayford Stores

The following ratios have been calculated for Bayford Stores for the years 2005 and 2006.

	2005	2006
Gross profit margin	35%	33.3%
Mark-up	53.8%	50%
Rate of stock turnover	12 times	14 times
Net profit margin	16%	18%
Wages and salaries to turnover	34%	37%
Return on capital employed	18%	17%
Net current assets ratio	2.3 : 1	1.9 : 1
Liquid capital ratio	1.5 : 1	1.4 : 1
Debtor collection period	36 days	31 days
Creditor payment period	33 days	34 days

Table 9.2 *Calculated ratios*

Additional information:

Turnover was £310,000 in 2005 and £340,000 in 2006

Benchmarks for this business sector:

■ Net current assets ratio 1.8:1
■ Liquid capital ratio 1.4:1

Assess the performance of Bayford Stores comparing 2006 with 2005

Strengths

Turnover has increased substantially between the two years (by £30,000). This could be due to the reduction in the gross profit margin (by 1.7%) and mark-up percentages (by 3.8%) which may imply that selling prices have been reduced giving the business a more competitive edge.

The rate of stock turnover has increased (from 12 to 14 times a year). This could have resulted from the increase in turnover between the two years; it might also be due to a reduction in average stock perhaps saving storage costs.

The net profit margin percentage has increased (by 2%). This may just have resulted from the increased turnover, but could also have resulted from some efficiencies in controlling expenses.

Both liquidity ratios have fallen slightly and are now nearer (in the case of the net current assets ratio) or exactly in line with (in the case of the liquid capital ratio) the sector averages. This suggests that liquid resources are being managed more efficiently.

The debtors collection period has decreased (by 5 days) implying greater credit control. At the same time the creditor payment period has lengthened (by 1 day) which may have helped conserve the

business's liquid resources. Whereas creditors were being paid more frequently than amounts due from debtors were being collected, this position has now been reversed.

Weaknesses

Despite the improvement in the net profit percentage, wages and salaries have increased (by 3%) out of proportion to the increase in sales. This could imply that this cost has not been so effectively controlled.

The return on capital employed has fallen (by 1%) despite increased net profits. The implication is that there has been an increase in capital invested in the company and that capital is now earning slightly less profits than previously, so resources are not being used as effectively as before.

Final judgement and recommendation

Overall the business's performance has improved since 2005 with increased sales, net profits and more efficient liquidity ratios. However, the owner should address the slight decline in one key ratio, i.e. the return on capital employed.

■ Gearing

What does the gearing ratio tell you about a limited company's performance?

The **gearing ratio** measures:

- how a company is financed
- finance on which there is a fixed return compared to all of a company's finance.

If the percentage is *above 50%*, this tells you that the company:

- is high-geared
- has high amounts of fixed-return financing in relation to all financing
- will be able to pay interest/dividends on the fixed-return financing reasonably easily if the company is doing well in terms of profits
- may have difficulty in meeting its commitment to pay interest/ dividends if the company is not doing well and profits are low, or a loss is being made
- may find it difficult to borrow more, because it already has a relatively high amount of fixed-return finance.

If the percentage is *below 50%*, this tells you that the company:

- is low-geared
- has low amounts of fixed-return financing in relation to all financing
- will tend to experience very few problems in meeting commitments to pay interest/dividends
- may find it relatively easy to borrow additional funds, because it currently has low levels of borrowing.

Further means of interpreting the gearing ratio

High-geared companies are often referred to as high-risk companies; conversely low-geared companies are often referred to as low-risk companies. The risk element refers to the company's vulnerability if profits are low or non-existent.

Stakeholders will be interested in the gearing ratio for a variety of reasons. For example, an ordinary shareholder will be concerned about the impact on profits, and therefore dividend payments, if a company becomes high-geared.

Illustration

Assessing Benetex plc's gearing ratio

Benetex plc's gearing ratios over a three-year period were as follows:

	Year 1	Year 2	Year 3
Gearing	70%	50%	30%

Table 9.3 *Gearing ratios*

Basic observation:

- the geaing percentage has fallen over the 3-year period
- the company has moved from being high-geared to low-geared.

Interpretation:

The reduction in the gearing ratio means that the company has reduced its financing from debentures or other long-term loans and/or from preference shares. Alternatively, the reduction in the ratio could be due to increased financing from ordinary shares and/or building up reserves. The company will now be less vulnerable if profits fall because it has a lower proportion of fixed-return finance than previously. The company will find it is in a better position to borrow funds if this is necessary. The decline in the gearing ratio means the company has moved from being a high-risk to a low-risk company.

Learning outcomes

As a result of studying this topic, you should now be able to:

- prepare a report on the financial performance of a sole trader or a limited company with a focus on profitability and liquidity

- analyse the performance of a business comparing results over a period of years

- assess the performance of a business comparing it with other similar businesses or with benchmarks for businesses in the same sector

- evaluate a business's performance by assessing strengths and weaknesses in performance

- make recommendations as to how a business's performance could be improved

AQA Examination-style questions

✓ **1**   The following ratios have been calculated as a result of analysing the trading and profit and loss accounts of Gorbrin Ltd for the last three years.

	Year ended 31 December		
	2005	**2006**	**2007**
Gross profit margin	40%	38%	37%
Mark up	67%	61%	59%
Rate of stock turnover	11 times	13 times	14 times
Net profit margin	12%	11%	10%
Wages and salaries/turnover	5%	7%	9%
Other overheads/turnover	13%	12.5%	12%

Gorbrin Ltd's turnover in each of these years was:

2005   £620,000
2006   £790,000
2007   £980,000

Comment on the company's performance over the three-year period.

For each ratio:

(a)   describe the trend and state whether this a strength or weakness

(b)   explain what may have caused the change and the implications of the change.

2   An analysis of the balance sheets of Gorbrin Ltd at 31 December 2005, 2006 and 2007 produced the following ratios.

	Balance Sheet at 31 December		
	2005	**2006**	**2007**
Return on capital employed	14%	16%	18%
Net current assets ratio	2.2 : 1	2.3 : 1	2.4 : 1
Liquid capital ratio	1.3 : 1	1.2 : 1	1.1 : 1
Debtor collection period	34 days	36 days	37 days
Creditor payment period	33 days	32 days	31 days
Gearing	40%	50%	60%

Note: benchmarking data for other companies in this sector shows that the average net current assets ratio is 2.2 : 1, and the average liquid capital ratio is 1.1 : 1.

Comment on the company's performance over the three-year period.

For each ratio:

(a)   describe the trend and state whether this a strength or weakness

(b)   explain what may have caused the change and the implications of the change.

3   ACC4 January 2002

The following is an extract from the trial balance of Williamson Ltd as at 30 November 2007.

	Dr £	Cr £
Stock at 1 December 2006	22,000	
Debtors	50,080	
Balance at bank		2,000
Trade creditors		48,000
Credit sales		356,705
Credit purchases	350,400	

Additional information:

- Stock at 30 November 2007 was valued at £33,000.
- A trade debtor has notified Williamson Ltd that they have gone into liquidation. This debtor does not expect to be able to pay any of the outstanding debt of £7,080. No adjustment has been made for this.

Required

(a)   Define the term 'working capital'.

(b)   Calculate the following, showing your workings. State the formula used:
- the net current assets ratio
- the acid test ratio
- the debtor collection period
- the creditor payment period.

(c)   Analyse the effect on Williamson Ltd's liquidity and its liquidity ratios caused by:
- writing off the bad debt
- increasing the value of stock over the year.

4   ACC4 June 2004

Supps Supermarket is located in a small seaside town. The owner, Ernie Supps, regularly meets with his friend Sid Plates, a retailer in crockery, whose outlet is based in the same town.

During one of their meetings the two friends discussed the financial ratios prepared for each business for the six months ending 31 December 2007.

The ratios were as follows:

	Supps Supermarket	Sid Plates
Net current assets ratio	1.1: 1	1.2: 1
Acid test	0.65: 1	0.9: 1
Net profit to turnover	6%	2%
Rate of stock turnover	29 times	6 times
Return on capital employed	2%	7%

Required

(a)   Define working capital.

(b)   State the formula used to calculate the acid test ratio.

(c)   Explain **two** possible reasons for the difference between the acid test ratios of the two businesses.

(d)   Explain **two** possible consequences to the employees of Supps Supermarket if action is not taken to improve the liquidity ratios.

(e)   Write a brief report to Sid Plates:

- analysing his business's ratios

- suggesting **two** ways in which his business's performance could be improved.

10 Introduction to budgeting and budgetary control

So far all your work in accounting has been about recording financial information about past events. However, accounting techniques can also be useful in preparing forecasts of the future for individual businesses, so that owners and managers can make much more informed and effective decisions to improve their business's performance. You will develop an understanding of the advantages that businesses can gain from preparing budgets, but also develop an awareness of the limitations of this procedure. In this chapter you will learn how budgeting techniques can be used to predict future cash balances by producing cash budgets. Your existing knowledge of cash transactions will help you understand how businesses receive and spend money. Your understanding of credit transactions will help you understand why there will be a delay in receiving cash from debtors and a delay in making payments to creditors. Your understanding of depreciation will also be useful, because you will be quick to realise that depreciation has no effect on a business's cash resources.

Case study

'Bookworm'

'Bookworm' is owed by Katy Thomas. It is a small second-hand bookshop that Katy opened in January 2005 and it is located in a small market town. Katy is a great book lover and she has a real flair for getting customers interested in her second-hand books. However, she has relatively little financial knowledge or experience.

Link

For more information on budgets, see A2 Module 4.

The advantages of budgeting

Why businesses prepare budgets: the advantages of budgeting

- Budgets ensure that business activity has been carefully *planned* by the owners or managers.
- They also provide a basis for *monitoring* actual activity against forecasts.
- They enable expenditure to be *controlled* more effectively.
- Budgets ensure that business activity is *co-ordinated*.

Illustration

The benefits Katy will gain from preparing budgets for 'Bookworm'

When Katy started the business she approached her bank for a loan. She was required to prepare a cash budget in support of her loan application. This was a condition of lending Katy some of the funds she needed to get the business started.

Key terms

Planning: in budgeting, the idea of using objectives and targets as the basis for determining what should happen.

Monitoring: in budgeting, the idea of comparing what actually happens with what has been forecast and investigating why differences occur.

Control: in budgeting, the idea of setting limits to expenditure so that the business as a whole will function well.

Co-ordination: in budgeting, the idea of bringing together a range of factors when determining the timing of events.

Planning: In order to prepare her cash budget, Katy had to carefully consider what her business objectives should be. She started by thinking about how much drawings she would need to take out of the business each month in order to finance her living expenses. She also worked out how much she would have to pay in business rent, rates, insurance and other expenses. Next she considered how much she was likely to pay for stocks of second-hand books and the levels of mark-up that would attract, rather than deter, customers. As a result of these considerations, she was able to set targets for monthly sales. She had to work through these plans several times over to ensure that she would be able to meet her objectives with realistic figures.

Monitoring: having planned levels of sales and expenditure of running costs, stocks and drawings, Katy was in position to prepare a detailed cash budget. As she began trading, she was able to compare actual sales figures, and actual expenditure, with her detailed plan. She found this every useful, because she was able to quickly spot when actual events were different from her forecasts. For example, in June 2005 she noted that sales were much higher than predicted. She investigated why this was so and found that she had not realised an annual festival would be taking place in the town centre where 'Bookworm' was located, and this brought in many tourists who visited the bookshop. As a result of this careful comparison she was able to adjust her budget for future years to take account of the June festival. In other words, Katy carefully monitored actual events against forecasts and where they did not match up, she took the trouble to investigate the reasons.

Control: Katy's carefully planned cash budget set limits to how much she could spend each month on running costs and stock. For example, her cash budget showed clearly that she could afford to spend £3,500 on new stock in September 2005. This amount of expenditure would be sufficient to keep the bookshop well stocked without causing the bank account to be overdrawn. In other words, the cash budget, in setting limits for each type of expenditure, controlled her spending.

Co-ordination: Katy's carefully prepared cash budget resulted not just from careful planning, but also giving some thought to the timing of various events. For example, Katy quickly came to realise that if she was to base her plans on realistic levels of sales and build in to the budget the required amount of drawings, she would not be able to furnish and equip her business as thoroughly as she would like in the early years. In other words, she had to bring together all the factors involved in establishing a successful business in her cash budget and this required some careful scheduling of events. Her budget was, therefore, carefully co-ordinated.

Further benefits of budgeting

In large organisations, budgeting often involves many of the employees in the planning stages. Where this is done effectively, *staff motivation* often increases. Staff feel they have had a part to play in setting the targets that they are to reach and, as a result, become more determined to reach these targets.

Budgets are also an effective means of *communicating* targets throughout an organisation from managers to staff. Where there is a comprehensive budgeting system in place, individuals are able to identify how their work for a part of the organisation fits in with the whole.

Disadvantages of budgeting

What are the potential disadvantages of budgeting?

- Budgets can act as strait-jackets and as a result important but unexpected opportunities can be turned down.
- Budgets can de-motivate staff if the targets set are too challenging of if the staff feel the targets have been imposed upon them.
- On the other hand, budgets may be rather undemanding, so that targets set can be easily reached and the business's potential not fully realised.

Illustration

The possible drawbacks of preparing budgets for 'Bookworm'

Katy's cash budget for November 2005 showed that she could afford to spend £4,100 on stocks of second-hand books. In early November she attended a monthly book auction. At the auction a rare opportunity arose to acquire a considerable number of second-hand books being sold off really cheaply by the owner of a large country house for £9,000. Katy, however, kept to her budget limit of £4,100. Katy was probably wrong to feel constrained by her budget, because she could have acquired valuable stock at a low price. Maybe she would have been overdrawn at the bank, but in the longer term she might have a good profit on the additional stock purchased at a good price.

Activity

Matt Bennett has decided that it could be a good idea for a cash budget to be prepared. Identify:

a   four benefits that could arise from preparing a cash budget

b   two drawbacks that could arise from preparing a cash budget.

Preparing cash budgets

How do businesses prepare cash budgets?

Cash budgets are usually prepared on a month-by-month basis. The main elements in the budget are:

- *forecast opening balance* for the first month in the budget period
- *forecast opening balances* for the second and subsequent months in the budget period (these balances will result from carrying forward the closing balance from the previous month)
- *forecast receipts* from cash sales, from debtors paying for credit sales relating to the previous month or months, additional borrowing, additional capital investment, interest and/or rent received, cash received from the sale of fixed assets
- *forecast payments* for purchases, to creditors paying for the purchases relating to the previous month or months, for expenses, drawings (or dividend payments), loan repayments, purchases of fixed assets, etc.
- *closing balances* for each month to be calculated as follows: opening balance + receipts for the month – payments for the month.

Key terms

Cash budget: a plan showing estimated future receipts and payments that enables possible surpluses or shortages of cash to be identified.

The figures to be entered will result from the setting of carefully thought out objectives and planning of future activities.

One of the main points of preparing a cash budget is to establish what the closing cash balance will be each month, based on the owner's or management's plans. If the cash budget reveals that there will a shortage of cash in any particular month, then suitable action can be taken to ensure the funds will be available to cover the shortage (for example, by arranging a bank overdraft) or by adjusting the plans to avoid the shortage (for example, postponing the purchase of a fixed asset). On the other hand, if there is surplus cash in any month, action can be taken to ensure

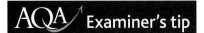

that the surplus is invested to provide interest, or the budget plans are adjusted to make better use of cash resources in some other way. A final version of the cash budget will be useful evidence of careful management and expertise, should the owner wish to apply for a bank loan. It will also provide evidence that the business can afford to make monthly interest payments and, of course, repay the loan.

Illustration

Preparing a cash budget for 'Bookworm'

Katy Thomas has ambitious plans for 'Bookworm' for the four-month period ending 31 December 2007. She will continue to purchase some stock for cash, but has also arranged credit terms with a new supplier of second-hand books. She has also agreed to offer credit terms to a few of her more important customers.

Her detailed plans are as follows:

1   Cash balances on 1 September 2007 are expected to be £3,800.

2   Total monthly sales for the 5-month period August to December 2007 are forecast to be:

	£
August	5,000
September	5,400
October	5,600
November	4,800
December	6,400

80% of all sales will be for cash. Remaining sales will be on credit terms.

Katy Thomas plans to offer one month's credit.

3   Cash purchases during the budget period are planned to be:

	£
September	1,600
October	1,100
November	3,200
December	2,600

4   The new supplier of second-hand books has offered her two months' credit and this arrangement is due to begin in September 2007. Katy plans to make the following credit purchases from this supplier:

	£
September	800
October	1,200
November	1,300
December	900

5   Katy has arranged with her landlord to pay rent of £800 per month quarterly in advance. Payments are due on 1 February, 1 May, etc.

6   Other expenses payments are forecast as follows:

	£
September	600
October	700
November	1,000
December	1,400

7 Katy plans to have monthly cash drawings of £2,200.

8 Katy will repay the bank loan at the rate of £300 per month. The last instalment is due in November 2007.

BOOKWORM CASH BUDGET

for each of the 4 months ending 31 December 2007

	September	October	November	December
	£	£	£	£
RECEIPTS				
Cash sales	4,320	4,480	3,840	5,120
Credit sales	1,000	1,080	1,120	960
	5,320	5,560	4,960	6,080
Cash purchases	1,600	1,100	3,200	2,600
Credit purchases			800	1,200
Rent			2,400	
Other expenses	600	700	1,000	1,400
Drawings	2,200	2,200	2,200	2,200
Loan repayment	300	300	300	
	4,700	4,300	9,900	7,400
Opening balance	3,800	4,420	5,680	740
Total receipts	5,320	5,560	4,960	6,080
	9,120	9,980	10,640	6,820
Total payments	4,700	4,300	9,900	7,400
Closing balance	4,420	5,680	740	-580

Figure 10.1 *Cash budget*

AQA Examiner's tip

Timing of receipts and payments: whereas cash sales and cash purchases can be entered in a cash budget with relative ease, receipts from debtors and payments to creditors will need a more cautious approach, for example:

■ if creditors allow one month's credit, the entry for creditors in the cash budget for a particular month will relate to the credit purchases made in the previous month

■ if debtors are allowed two months' credit, the entry for debtors in the cash budget for a particular month will relate to credit sales made two months previously.

■ Background knowledge

Background knowledge: many private individuals prepare budgets. For example, students in higher education, aware that finances are likely to be difficult and that there could be a real anxiety about building up substantial debts, are often advised to prepare cash budgets. There is the possibility of gaining all the advantages listed above from this activity if it is undertaken with care, but, of course, some of the disadvantages could arise, too.

⚐✔ *Learning outcomes*

As a result of studying this chapter, you should now be able to:

■ explain why businesses prepare budgets

■ evaluate budgeting by considering the possible advantages and disadvantages of this process

■ prepare cash budgets

 Examination-style questions

☑ **1** Rakesh is planning to open a retail outlet. His bank has asked him to prepare a cash budget for each of the first four months he will be in business, January to April 2009. Rakesh has submitted the following forecasts.

1 He will introduce capital of £50,000 paid into a bank account in the business's name on 1 January 2009.

Sales (all cash) will be as follows:

	£
January	18,900
February	21,000
March	22,400
April	24,000

2 Purchases will be as follows:

	£
January	12,000
February	13,000
March	14,000
April	15,000

Rakesh estimates that 10% of each month's purchases will be paid for in cash; the remaining purchases will be made on credit. He has arranged one month's credit terms with his suppliers.

3 Expense payments will be as follows:

	£
January	2,400
February	2,700
March	3,000
April	2,900

4 Rakesh plans to withdraw £2,000 per month for personal living expenses.

5 Capital expenditure will amount to £48,000. £40,000 will be paid in January 2009 and the remainder in March 2009.

Required

Prepare the cash budget for Rakesh's business for each of the 4 months ending 30 April 2009.

 Examiner's tip

Layout of cash budgets: there are a variety of ways of setting out a cash budget. All conventional layouts are accepted. You are advised to get used to using more than one layout, as the examination question may provide a particular template for your answer.

RAKESH
Cash budget for each of the four months ending 30 April 2009

	January	February	March	April
	£	£	£	£
RECEIPTS				
Capital introduced				
Cash sales				
PAYMENTS				
Cash purchases				
Credit purchases				
Expenses				
Drawings				
Capital expenditure				
Opening balance	0			
Total receipts				
Total payments				
Closing balance				

2   ACC4 June 2001

Sunshine Ltd sells beach buckets and spades.

The forecast information for the six months ending 31 October 2008 is:

	May	June	July	August	September	October
	£000	£000	£000	£000	£000	£000
Sales	16	20	26	28	24	20
Purchases	12	16	18	14	12	10
Overheads	4	8	8	8	8	4

Additional information:

1   On average 20% of each month's sales are expected to be for cash. A further 60% will be given on one month's credit. The remainder will be given two months' credit. All monies should be received when due.

2   The increase in overheads arises from the employment of casual staff. The overheads are paid in the month in which they occur.

3   Suppliers are expected to allow one month's credit.

4   The cash at bank balance at 1 July 2008 is £7,200 overdrawn.

Required

Prepare a detailed forecast month by month cash budget for the four months ending 31 October 2002.

(i)   Assess the cash position of Sunshine Ltd at 31 October 2008.

(ii) Recommend **one** way the company could improve its cash position.

Sunshine Ltd
Cash budget for four months ending 31 October 2008

	July £	Aug £	Sept £	Oct £
Sales – cash				
– 1 month				
– 2 months				
Purchases				
Overheads				
Net inflow/outflow				
Opening balance				
Closing balance				

3 ACC7 June 2005

Sam Grieves has been running his own barber's shop for many years.

The price of a haircut is £8. Sam employs one assistant at £8 per hour. Sam and his assistant each complete three haircuts per hour, five hours a day and six days a week.

The fixed overheads are £880 per week.

Sam needs to withdraw £400 per week for his own living expenses.

Sam decides to raise the price of a haircut for an adult to £10, but reduce the price for children under 12 years to £6. He knows that 75% of his customers are adults.

During the next four weeks, his assistant wishes to go abroad for two weeks with his family. This will be paid leave. Sam will not have an assistant for weeks 2 and 3, but he will complete three extra haircuts per day.

AQA Examiner's tip

Take care with the heading for a cash budget. The following points are important:

- inclusion of the name of the business
- clear statement about the time period being covered
- use of the word 'ending' rather than ended, because the budget is for a future period.

Sam currently has a loan of £3000. At the start of week 1, Sam has £500 in the bank and wishes to use any surplus cash to pay off his loan at the end of week 4, without going overdrawn. He realises that for weeks 2 and 3, his income will be reduced, and so he will reduce his own living expenses to £350 for each of these two weeks.

Required

(a) Calculate the maximum number of haircuts that are completed at the barber's shop per week.

(b) Prepare a cash budget for Sam for each of the four weeks.

Impact of ICT on accounting

Nowadays it is very unusual to find anyone keeping financial records manually. Computer technology, and particularly the development of specialised accounting software packages and, of course, spreadsheets, have revolutionised the way in which financial records are kept. In this chapter you will develop an understanding of the immense advantages these technological changes have made to business accounting, but also be able to reflect on some potential drawbacks. You will not be expected to demonstrate any skills in the use of computers or software packages. However, it is likely that, since you have probably used spreadsheets, you will find you are able to understand the contents of this chapter relatively easily. You will learn how to apply your understanding of the advantages and disadvantages of computerisation from various points of view such as that of the owner of the business or the business's employees.

The advantages of computerised accounting records

Why have computerised accounting records?

- **Greater accuracy**: computer processes are automatic and are, therefore, error free. Human error is still possible, of course, but this is limited to the potential to make mistakes when inputting information or formulas.

- **Greater speed:** computer processes, such as calculating, are virtually instantaneous.

- **Simultaneous updating** of records follows from making just one entry.

- **Improved accessibility**: it is possible to find information much more quickly.

- **More information available:** it is possible to produce specific reports on key aspects of running the business because data can be analysed at great speed.

- **Cut in staff costs**: because so much of the work in recording financial information is done automatically, it is possible that fewer staff will be required to keep records, leading to a savings in wages.

Case study

'Bliss Chocolates'

Ryoma is the owner of a chain of retail outlets based in several shopping centres. These shops sell high-quality chocolates and are called 'Bliss Chocolates'. Ryoma manages the business himself, but he employs shop assistants at each branch.

Illustration

Bliss Chocolates acquires a computerised accounting system

Ryoma purchased a computer system and appropriate hardware a few years after opening 'Bliss Chocolates'. He found that the change from using manual methods made a great difference to the way he ran his business. With the accounting software, all that was necessary was to just enter the details from source documents such as suppliers' invoices, paying-in slip counterfoils, etc., and detailed accounts were produced automatically. He was also able to produce a range of important reports on his business automatically and at any time he chose, for example:

- trial balance
- detailed list of suppliers, amounts outstanding including an analysis of when each creditor was last paid
- final accounts showing profit for the business as a whole
- final accounts showing the turnover and profit and loss at each branch.

As a result he felt he had a much better idea of how his business was performing, and that he was in a much better position to make important decisions. For example, he was able to see week-by-week and month-by-month just how well each retail outlet was performing.

He also used the accounting software to produce:

- payroll records including pay slips for his shop assistants
- stock control records that would help him make sure products were re-ordered in a timely fashion for any branch of his business
- a fixed asset register providing a comprehensive record of important information about each of the business's fixed assets.

Ryoma found spreadsheets very valuable for preparing cash budgets. He found it was easy to try out a variety of scenarios with the spreadsheet producing new cash budgets instantly. As a result he could keep track of the impact of any changes to his plans for the business, producing more and more variations in budgets until he was satisfied with the results.

He was aware that if he chose to sell on credit, the accounting software would produce sales invoices. He would also be able to generate reports on debtors that would detail how much was outstanding and for how long accounts had been unpaid. He appreciated that these reports could help identify likely bad debts.

■ Activity

Explain why accounting packages are faster and more accurate than manual accounting methods.

■ Activity

Explain why spreadsheets are particularly useful for preparing cash budgets.

■ Disadvantages of computerised accounting systems

What are the disadvantages of having a computerised accounting system?

- **Capital expenditure:** the cost of the equipment and software can be high and the economic life of computer systems can be quite short. It may also be necessary to have software tailored for particular needs and this can also be expensive. Some computer software could have to be updated at frequent intervals.
- *Training costs:* if staff are inexperienced in using software they will need to be trained. When software updates come through, retraining may be necessary. Some staff could find the prospect of training alarming. On the other hand, staff who are skilled in the use of accounting software will be in demand and may be able to command higher salaries. So introducing computerised accounting records could be seen as an opportunity by some employees.
- *Staff morale:* the introduction of computer systems may lead to staff cuts that in turn could affect staff morale.
- *Risk of data loss and security breaches:* computer systems can be vulnerable to 'crashing', viruses and hacking.

Illustration

Bliss Chocolates experiences some disadvantages from having a computerised accounting system

Ryoma's capital expenditure on the computer system was high. He paid for a network of computers, their installation and software in the form of a specialised software package that included payroll and stock-control facilities. He also paid to have the software tailored to his need to produce detailed information about each branch of the business. One of his part-time employees who had maintained the financial records did not feel able to cope with change to computerised records and left the business. This employee was not replaced. The change in staffing unsettled some of the other employees. Ryoma paid for the other finance staff to be trained in the use of the software. Apart from the cost of the training, there was the difficulty of the transition period from manual records to computerised records. Ryoma was advised that it would be wise to keep both systems in operation for a short period during this period of transition. The cost of maintaining the system also proved high. There were a number of occasions he had to call out specialist help when problems arose with operating the system. Ryoma also found that once his staff were trained the risk of losing them increased simply because they had gained marketable skills.

AQA Examiner's tip

In a question requiring an evaluation it is important to focus on both the benefits and drawbacks of the proposal. As the question demands, all the points you make should be from the viewpoint of staff. Remember to give a clear recommendation at the end of your answer with a concise justification.

■ Activity

Identify two reasons why staff morale might be adversely affected by introducing a computerised accounting system.

Learning outcomes

As a result of studying this chapter, you should now be able to:

- explain the advantages and disadvantages of computerisation in regard to accounting and financial record keeping
- explain some specific computer applications that benefit businesses
- assess the impact of computerisation of accounting functions from the viewpoint of the owner of the business and from the viewpoint of employees

AQA Examiner's tip

It is important to note that Question 2 is specifically about the sales ledger. Each part of the answer should, therefore, relate to the sales ledger if it is to score maximum marks.

 # Examination-style questions

1 What are the main benefits and drawbacks of having a computerised accounting system?

2 ACC1 January 2006

Since Janice Booth introduced a mail-order facility, her business has expanded significantly. She is concerned, however, about the possibility of non-payment by debtors. She is considering investing in computer software to help manage her sales ledger.

Required

Identify and explain **three** ways in which the management of her sales ledger would benefit from computerisation.

3 ACC1 June 2002

The financial manager of R Masters proposes to introduce an updated computer for the accounting functions of the office, but the personnel manager is worried about the reaction of the staff to this change.

Required

Evaluate the proposal to introduce an updated computer from the point of view of the accounting staff.

Examination skills

Probably almost all of us have sat down at some time in an examination room, opened the exam paper and had some kind of bad experience, for example:

- 'I cannot remember how to do a question on that topic'
- 'I don't really know what I was supposed to do to answer that question'
- 'I don't think I have read the question carefully enough'
- 'I am going to run out of time'

Having worked hard through your course of study, you will, of course, be anxious to avoid any of these problems. There are probably two key things that could really help you do well and perhaps better than you might expect: being well prepared, of course, and gaining a good understanding of how the examination works.

Preparation during your course of study

Getting organised

Do you keep your homework answers, class handouts, model answers and class notes carefully? Could you find an answer to a question on a key topic easily? Could you find a model answer to that same question? The point of these questions is that when it comes to preparing for a test or for the final examination, you will need to be able to find these documents easily so that you get on to the task of revising without wasting any time.

Study skills

As well as working on all the new accounting topics and answering questions, have you also given some thought to how you learn best? For example, some students find it difficult to remember the correct order for shares and reserves on a company's balance sheet. Have you developed any memorising techniques that work for you and enable you to recall factual information relatively easily? Many students make up a memorable phrase or saying to help them with this sort of task. How about 'Oliver (ordinary shares) plays (preference shares) chess (capital reserves) regularly (revenue reserves)' as an example. Well, this phrase may not be memorable for you, but make up another alternative one and make it as silly as you like!

The idea of mnemonics, as illustrated in the previous paragraph, is probably familiar to you. But what about these other ideas . . .?

Marking your own work:

Do you regularly mark your own work against a model answer or the mark scheme provided by AQA, or do you pair up with someone else and mark each other's work? If you carry out this activity regularly then you are likely to get to really understand how you can earn marks in the examination, but more than that you can focus your attention on what you did well, but also, of course, on what went wrong. There is much research to show that students who regularly 'self-assess' (mark your own work) or 'peer assess' (pair up with someone and mark each other's work) significantly improve their performance in the subjects they are studying.

'Repairing' your answers:

Assuming you, or someone else, has just marked some work you have done, do you take a little time to focus on what went wrong? Again there is considerable evidence that students who regularly take a careful look at any part of an answer that went wrong and take some actions make substantial progress, often well beyond the progress that the individual expects can be made. The idea here is that you use a model answer to help you understand what you should have done when some part of a computational answer is incorrect. Take the trouble to write out a note on your marked work about what you should have done using the evidence in the model answer, and ensure that you understand how the model answer was achieved (perhaps with the help of the teacher or a fellow student). By the way, don't worry about making your piece of work look a bit messy! The ideal would be if you could say to yourself 'if I did this question again, I am confident I could get those difficult bits right'. Then, what about prose answers. Most students of accounting find prose answers rather difficult to do well. Again, use this idea of 'repairing' answers to help you make progress. In the case of a prose answer, this means noting on your own piece of work points made in the model answer that you omitted, or did not express very well. You will need to do this regularly throughout the course, but once again the evidence is that students who get into the habit of regularly using model answers in this way make considerable progress and over time begin to build up real confidence in preparing prose answers based on a good understanding of the points that they should include.

Monitoring your own progress

Many of you who are studying accounting in a school or college will have been provided with information about how well you should perform in this subject based on your performance in GCSEs. Perhaps you have been given information so that you work this out for yourself, or perhaps you have just been given what is often called a target grade. You could well, of course, have decided what level of performance you wish to obtain any way, never mind the target grade set by someone else. The question is: do you regularly monitor your own performance against one or all of these targets? Perhaps you do this in discussions with your tutor or subject teacher. Regularly checking on how well you are doing against your expectations can be valuable in helping you maintain the level of progress you need to make.

Examination practice

Have you tried plenty of past examination questions? If you are to be thoroughly prepared for the examination you do need to make sure you have tried past questions on every key topic in the examination. Have you given enough attention to both computational and prose questions? Don't forget the balance; there will be a fair proportion of both types of question in the examination for both AS modules. You will also find it helpful to ensure you answer these questions fully and with great attention to matters of presentation. For example, make a point of using proper headings for financial statements and don't get into the habit of cutting corners to save time. You need to go into the exam not having to think too hard about how best to present answers; this should be second nature to you at this stage.

■ Revising for the examinations

As the examination for each unit draws near you will be thinking about the best way to revise. Just how much revision is done and how frequently it is done will, of course, vary from one student to another. In accounting it is important that a substantial amount of your revision time is spent actually answering questions, so that you ensure you are skilled in actually carrying out accounting techniques, or that you remember key points to make in a variety of questions requiring a prose response. You might find it useful to make a checklist of all the main topics in each of the AS modules and work your way through the list finding questions to try on each item. If you have organised your work carefully you should be able to find a relevant question, an answer that you have produced yourself, a model answer or the exam mark scheme for each item on your checklist. If you feel confident about a topic just try the trickier parts of the question again, avoiding looking at the model answer unless you really get stuck. There is no need to produce carefully presented answers at this stage, unless you really want to; you will probably be more concerned to make the best use of your precious revision time, so for once cut corners, and perhaps produce key points for questions requiring a prose response rather than full answers. If you are less sure about a topic, be prepared to spend more time on it. Try working through the entire question, rather than just selected elements. Again, have a model answer around to help you when you get stuck. In the end you will find that actually answering questions will help you recover all the skills you had developed far more quickly than just looking through your notes and looking at your answers to past questions.

■ How the examination works

If you understand how the examination works it is very unlikely you will experience any surprises when you actually sit down to do the exam.

The structure of the examination paper

The following table sets out some key points about each of the two AS module assessment units (i.e. examinations). You will see that the papers have almost identical structures.

Questions about the structure of the examination	Unit 1	Unit 2
How long is the exam?	1 hour 30 minutes	1 hour 30 minutes
How many questions will I have to answer?	Four compulsory questions	Four compulsory questions
Will there be a choice of questions?	No	No
Will each question carry equal marks?	No, the questions will be of varying length and have varying numbers of tasks	No, the questions will be of varying length and have varying numbers of tasks
How many marks on each paper?	80	80
What is the likely balance between questions requiring a computational response and those requiring a prose response?	Approximately 60 marks for 'computational' questions and 20 marks for 'prose' questions	Approximately 55 marks for 'computational' questions and 25 marks for 'prose' questions

What are the examiners trying to assess?

Examination papers are designed with great care to ensure that candidates have an opportunity to show what they can do. You will find that papers try to cover as much of the subject content in one paper as possible, for example. However, it would be almost impossible to write an examination paper that included tasks on every aspect of the specification. Over several papers, though, the aim will be to examine every part of the specification. You will find that the tasks for each question are designed to include some that most candidates are likely to find easy. Wherever possible, the examiner will try to start the paper off with a more straightforward question so that candidates have a chance to make a good start and settle their nerves a little. It is likely that the last tasks in a particular question will be harder for most candidates. The examiner will be keen to make sure that candidates who are likely to achieve a lower grade have a good opportunity to demonstrate some knowledge, understanding and skills, but will also be keen to include tasks which only the candidates who will achieve the higher grades are likely to be able to do well.

It will not be apparent to most candidates looking at the examination paper that the examiner has also tried to ask questions that test important 'educational' skills:

■ **knowledge and understanding** – meaning can you define terms, explain accounting techniques, ideas and concepts; do you know how to set out accounting statements, etc.

■ **application** – meaning can you demonstrate skill in applying what you know about accounting techniques and prepare financial records and statements for a particular business, etc.

■ **analysis and evaluation** – can you select information, organise the information in a useful way, draw conclusions from the information, explain your conclusions to others and produce a balanced argument about the strengths and weaknesses of a particular situation or process?

A general awareness of these types of questions will help you prepare effectively for the examination. Broadly speaking, almost all candidates can usually do quite well in regard to 'knowledge and understanding'; fewer candidates are as confident when it comes to applying the knowledge, understanding and skills, and fewer still do well at analysis and evaluation questions. Do bear this in mind, particularly if you are aiming for a high grade.

In the two AS module assessment units the balance of questions that test these skills is as follows:

Skill	Unit 1	Unit 2
Knowledge and understanding	40%	20%
Application	50%	50%
Analysis and evaluation	10%	30%

Getting the timing right

Examination papers are written so that candidates should be able to complete all the questions in the time allowed. Of course, part of the skill of accounting is being able to process data quickly, so that there is an expectation that candidates should not have to take an undue amount of time trying to take in all the information provided. If you have taken examination practice seriously, you will have got used to getting on with the tasks as soon as you can. All candidates, however, do need to make sure they are making best use of the time available. It would be very damaging to your overall result if you mistimed things so badly that, for example, you failed to answer one of the questions. Clearly, in these circumstances your potential mark will be scaled down considerably.

It is often a good idea to divide up the 90 minutes available to complete the exam between the questions in roughly the proportion of the marks available. Don't take too long over working this out in the exam room, of course; an approximate calculation will probably do. Here are two examples to show you how this could work.

Example 1:

Marks available for each question	Calculation	Time available for each question (approximately)
20	There are 80 marks on the paper and 90 minutes to complete the paper; so you need to score 1 mark every 1.125 minutes	22
24		26
10		11
26		30
80 marks	TOTAL MARKS AND TIME	90 minutes

Example 2:

Marks available for each question	Calculation	Time available for each question (approximately)
15	There are 80 marks on the paper and 90 minutes to complete the paper; so you need to score 1 mark every 1.125 minutes	17
23		25
31		36
11		12
80 marks	TOTAL MARKS AND TIME	90 minutes

With approximate timing worked out, try to keep with the time for each question as you write your answers. Remember that every time you exceed the time you have allocated you will have to speed up in another question to make up the time lost.

If things get a little desperate, despite all this careful planning, don't give up! Do your best to find ways of showing that you can demonstrate you have a good understanding of the task(s) that you think you may have to rush through. If they are tasks requiring a prose response, perhaps abandon writing full statements and offer the main points in a bulleted list. You will not score full marks for this type of answer, but you will gain credit for the amount of knowledge and understanding you are showing.

Key words in questions

Examiners use a number of words when setting questions such as 'state', 'explain', 'discuss'. The examiner has an expectation that each of these types of word will produce a particular kind of answer. Obviously, it is important for candidates to understand exactly what the examiner's expectations are. Look through the following list of key words used in examination questions in accounting.

You probably don't need reminding of the most common problem in examinations, i.e. the candidate did not read the question properly and so did not produce the required answer. Again, practice will help you get the balance of time spent reading questions carefully to actually answering the questions in the right proportion. So when the question says 'prepare a balance sheet extract showing . . .', spend enough time reading the question to note the word extract, otherwise, of course, you could end up wasting a lot of time producing a complete balance sheet!

Key term	What the examiner expects	Examples
Identify State	This type of question usually tests factual recall. You are not expected to write at length; just one word or a phrase will usually be sufficient.	Q: Identify the accounting concept that is used when valuing stocks A: Just one word required. i.e. 'prudence'
List	Again this type of question is concerned with factual recall and a few words at most are all that is usually expected.	Q: List three concepts that are used when valuing assets A: Again just words or phrases required, i.e. 'objectivity, cost, going concern'
Explain	This question is testing how much you really understand and so more is expected by the examiner. You will need to write several sentences at least. In one sentence you will need to convey that you have a basic understanding of the subject matter of the question. It will then be important to develop this answer further to score full marks. You will need, therefore, to add other statements in which you show that you have a good grasp of the background to the subject matter of the topic, that you can illustrate the points you have made, perhaps providing examples.	Q: Explain the accounting concept of consistency. A: Here several sentences required each demonstrating various degrees of understanding. The concept consistency requires businesses to use the same accounting methods and policies from one accounting period to the next (basic idea). This will ensure that valid comparisons can be made of one year's results with those for another year (showing further understanding). The user of accounts will, therefore, be able to make valid judgements and decisions based on the comparison (showing yet more understanding). For example, if a business adopts the straight-line method of depreciation, this method should be applied in each accounting period (providing an illustration or example that provides further evidence of understanding).

Prepare	This question will usually require accounting statements to be produced. This type of question is designed to test your knowledge of the correct layouts for various financial statements, your ability to work through the statements in the correct sequence and to select data, sometimes making calculations, from that provided. The setting for the question (i.e. the business that is the subject of the question) and occasionally the way some of the data is presented will be unfamiliar to you.	Q: Prepare a cash budget A: You will produce a cash budget using a conventional layout. Sometimes a template may be given
Calculate	This question will require you to select the correct data and use the correct arithmetical processes to produce a particular result. The question is likely to test your understanding of a particular accounting technique.	Q: Calculate the gearing ratio A: You will need to state the formula for this ratio; select the correct figures from all the data supplied; correctly divide (in this case) fixed-return finance by all finance, and finally present your answer in the correct form, i.e. a percentage
Discuss	This type of question requires you to demonstrate a full understanding of a topic by presenting arguments that either support or counter a particular course of action. You will be expected to give your final view and provide a justification for your view based on the arguments you have outlined.	Q: Discuss whether a sole trader should convert the business into a partnership A: Your answer should present the case for staying as a sole trader (i.e. an explanation of the benefits of being a sole trader) and the disadvantages of this type of business organisation. The answer should then explain the extent to which forming a partnership would overcome any of the difficulties of being a sole trader, and the extent to which being in partnership might produce new disadvantages. Your answer should end with a final judgement based on the arguments you have presented and include a concise justification for the view you have taken
Evaluate	This type of question requires you to weigh up the strengths and weaknesses of a particular accounting process or technique, or a particular course of action, or the performance of a business. You are expected to reach a final overall judgement, perhaps in the form of a recommendation or piece of advice. Your final judgement should be accompanied by a concise justification for your view.	Q: Evaluate a sole trader's decision to introduce a system of budgetary control A: Your answer will include an explanation of the benefits of introducing budgetary control. The best answers would include illustrations relevant to the particular business being considered. You should then provide an explanation of the possible disadvantages of budgetary control. Again include illustrations that relate to the business under consideration. Finally, you should express your overall view as to whether budgetary control should be introduced and provide a short justification

Getting the finer details right

If you look back through Chapters 1 to 11 you will recall that examiner tips have been included to help you produce the best answers possible in examinations. Many of these tips relate to particular topics, but here are some of the points made that might apply to a wide range of questions.

▓ Provide correct headings for all financial statements and avoid using any abbreviations

in the titles such as y/e, 31 Dec 07, p&l, etc. In addition, do make a point of naming the business concerned.

Examples of good practice:

Trading and Profit and Loss Account for the year ended 31 December 2007

Balance Sheet at 30 September 2007

Cash budget for each of the four months ending 30 November 2007

Provide workings to support the figures you use in answers to computation tasks. Unless the calculation is very straightforward, the person marking your script will need to know, step by step, how you reached your final figure. As you probably already know, there are often marks for each step in a calculating process, and without the evidence these marks may be not be allocated to you.

Examples of good practice:

Proposed ordinary shared dividend	£12,500

[5% × 500,000 shares of 50p each

= 5% × £250,000]

Depreciation of equipment

[30% × net book value (cost £40,000 less

existing depreciation £12,000)

= 30% × £28,000]   £8,400

Take some trouble to use the right technical terms in prose answers and the correct labels for subtotals in financial statements. If you have the knowledge and understanding don't hesitate to show off!

Examples of good practice:

On a company's balance sheet

Creditors: amounts falling due within one year (rather than current liabilities)

Depreciation is based on an assessment of the *economic life* of a fixed asset

(rather than 'depreciation is based on an estimate of how long the fixed asset will last')

In each examination four of the marks will be allocated to what is called the 'quality of written communication'. The person who marks your script will be looking for some particular points when awarding these marks:

Spelling: is your spelling generally good? It does not have to be perfect! Anyone can misspell a word, particularly under the pressure of completing an examination.

Punctuation: have you followed the usual conventions in regard to the use of punctuation?

Grammar: have you written in sentences and are these grammatically correct? Avoid a list of bulleted points in prose answers (except when you are really under pressure to complete a task). Again the odd slip-up will be considered acceptable.

Presentation: have you used conventional layouts for accounting statements, including reports and memoranda, and have you provided accurate headings, subheadings, etc?

Terminology: in prose answers have you used terms correctly and avoided using everyday language when there are specific words or phrases which are part of the language of accounting?

Glossary

'DEAD CLIC': a mnemonic to help remember the rules of Dr and Cr: **D**ebit, **E**xpenditure, **A**ssets, **D**rawings, **C**redit, **L**iabilities, **I**ncome, **C**apital

A

Accruals: expenses and revenues are matched for a time period when calculating profit

Annual general meeting: often called the AGM is the yearly company meeting that can be attended by shareholders

Assets: resources that are available for use by the business

Auditors' fees: the amount paid to those who check the accounting records. This item is an expense

Authorised capital: the maximum amount of capital the company can issue by way of shares

B

Bad debt recovered: an amount received from a debtor that has previously been written off

Bad debt written off: amount owed by a debtor that is irrecoverable

Balance sheet: a statement detailing all of the assets and liabilities of a business

Balancing off accounts: the process of calculating the balance between the debits and credits on a ledger account and carrying forward the balance into the next accounting period

Bank overdraft: a form of loan where the bank allows a customer to be overdrawn (make total payments in excess of total receipts) up to a specified limit

Bank statement: a printout issued by the bank detailing all receipts into the account, payments out of the account and a running balance

Bonus issue: the issue of additional shares to shareholders in proportion to their existing shareholders. No cash is paid for the additional shares. The issue is financed from company reserves, resulting in a re-structuring of the capital and reserves section of the balance sheet

Business entity: an accounting system that contains records of that organisation only

C

Cancelled cheque: a cheque drawn by the business and subsequently cancelled before payment

Capital: resources (cash or other assets) introduced by the owner to run the business

Capital employed: for a limited company this is made up of shares + reserves + long-term liabilities

Capital expenditure: money spent on fixed assets that is intended to benefit future financial periods

Capital reserve: profits that have been set aside and do not originate from the everyday trading activities of the company. Capital reserves cannot be distributed as dividends

Cash book: book of original entry recording cash and cheque payments and receipts. The cash book also has columns to record discount received and discount allowed

Cash budget: a plan showing estimated future receipts and payments that enables possible surpluses or shortages of cash to be identified

Cash discount: a reduction in the amount owing to a supplier in return for settling their bills early (e.g. payment within 14 days)

Cash receipts and till rolls: contains details of cash received

Cheque counterfoil: contains details of cheques drawn (date, payee and amount)

Consistency: accounting methods are applied in the same way in each accounting period

Contra entry: a cancellation of a debit balance with a credit balance in different books of account

Contra: An amount set off in the sales ledger account against the purchases ledger account of the same person(s)

Control: in budgeting, the idea of setting limits to expenditure so that the business as a whole will function well

Co-ordination: in budgeting, the idea of bringing together a range of factors when determining the timing of events

Corporation tax: tax on a company's profits

Cost: the price paid for the asset

Cost of sales: total purchases plus carriage inwards adjusted for opening and closing stock on hand

Credit note: a document detailing sales or purchase returns or an overcharge, together with reasons

Creditor payment period: is trade creditors in relation to credit purchases; the ratio is expressed as so many days

Creditors: amounts falling due after more than one year: a balance sheet subheading used for a company's long-term liabilities

Creditors: amounts falling due within one year: a balance sheet subheading used for a company's current liabilities

Current assets: company resources that are planned to be converted into cash within 12 months

Current liabilities: monies owed by the business due for repayment within twelve months

D

Debentures: loans to a company on which a fixed rate of interest is paid. The interest is an expense to be charged to the profit and loss account

Debtor collection period: trade debtors in relation to credit sales;

the ratio is expressed as so many days

Delivery note: a document detailing the goods that have been delivered by the supplier

Depreciation: the loss in value of a fixed asset over its useful economic life that is apportioned to financial periods. It is a non-cash expense

Direct debit: where authority is granted by the business to a third party for fixed or variable payments to be made at the request of that third party

Directors: the senior managers of a limited company; appointed by shareholders at the AGM

Directors' fees: the amount paid for the work done by directors. This item is an expense

Discount allowed: discount given to customers who settle bills promptly

Discount received: discount we receive from suppliers for settling our bills promptly

Drawings: funds withdrawn from the business by the owner for personal use

Equity shares: are ordinary shares

Estimated residual value: the estimated value of the asset at the end of its useful life

Estimated useful economic life: the estimated time that the business will continue to use the asset

Fixed assets: resources owned by the business intended for continuing use in running the business rather than for resale

G

Gearing: is fixed-return financing (preference shares and long-term liabilities) in relation to all sources of finance (shares, reserves and long-term liabilities); the ratio is expressed as a percentage

General journal: book of original entry recording non-routine transactions that do not appear in the other books of original entry

General ledger: a ledger containing all impersonal accounts

General reserve: part of the company's profits that has been set aside to indicate that it is likely to be retained within the company for the foreseeable future

Going concern: the assumption that a business will continue to trade for the foreseeable future

Gross profit margin: gross profit in relation to turnover (measured as a percentage)

Gross profit: the difference between sales and the cost of those sales

Income due: money that should have been received by a business from a debtor (such as a tenant) relating to the current financial period but that is yet to be received

Income received in advance: money received by a business from a debtor (such as a tenant) but that relates to the next financial period

Interim dividend: a half-yearly dividend

Invoice: a document detailing the goods or services supplied and the price paid

Issued capital: the amount of shares that the company has chosen to issue to date

Liabilities: monies owed by the business

Limited liability company: a form of organisation whose owners (or members) own shares and where the owners enjoy the benefit of having limited liability for the debts of the business. Companies have a separate existence from their owners

Limited liability: the responsibility of the owners of the business (shareholders) for the debts of the business is limited to the amount they have agreed to invest

Liquid capital ratio: is liquid capital in relation to current liabilities; the ratio is sometimes called the acid test ratio. This is an important measure of liquidity

Liquid capital: is current assets excluding stock

Liquidity: the ability of a business to access sufficient cash resources to pay its short-term liabilities

Long-term liabilities: monies owed by the business due for repayment at a time after 12 months

M

Mark-up: gross profit in relation to cost of sales (measured as a percentage)

Materiality: if the amount involved is relatively insignificant, then the usual accounting treatment of an item can be set aside

Monitoring: in budgeting, the idea of comparing what actually happens with what has been forecast and investigating why differences occur

Mortgage: a long-term loan, usually secured against assets

N

Net cost: initial cost of the asset less the estimated residual value at the end of the asset's useful economic life

Net current assets/liabilities: the difference between current assets and current liabilities

Net current assets ratio: is current assets in relation to current liabilities; the ratio is sometimes called the current ratio or the working capital ratio. This is an important measure of liquidity

Net loss: the final figure on the profit and loss account when the gross profit is *less than* the expenses that have been deducted from it

Net profit margin: net profit in relation to turnover (measured as a percentage)

Net profit: the final figure on the profit and loss account when the gross profit is *greater than* the expenses that have been deducted from it

Net realisable value: sale value less any costs necessary to incur a sale

Nominal accounts: a type of impersonal account relating to all non-real accounts

O

Objectivity: factual information is preferred because it is likely to be beyond dispute

Operating profit: profit before interest charges and tax (i.e. net profit + interest)

Order of liquidity: the order in which current assets are able to be turned into cash

Ordinary shares: shares that carry voting rights and have a variable dividend that is dependent on the amount of profits

Outstanding (uncleared) lodgements: bank deposits that have been recorded in the cash book but have not yet been processed by the bank

Overhead to turnover: each overhead in relation to turnover (measured as a percentage)

P

Partnership: where two or more individuals run a continuing business for profit

Par value; nominal value: the face value of a share

Paying in slip counterfoil: contains details on funds paid into the bank (date, source and amount)

Petty cash voucher: contains details of small cash payments made

Planning: in budgeting, the idea of using objectives and targets as the basis for determining what should happen

Preference shares: shares that have a fixed rate of dividend and normally have no voting rights

Private company: one in which only the founders of the company, their family, friends and employees can invest in shares

Profit after taxation: net profit for the year less the provision for corporation tax

Profit and loss account: calculates a business's net profit by deducting the expenses of running the business from the gross profit

Provision for doubtful debts: an amount set aside from profits to take account of the likelihood that some debtors will not be able to pay the amount due

Prudence: where there is doubt, asset and profit values are under- rather than overstated

Public company: one in which any member of the public can invest as shares are floated on the open market

Purchase day book: book of original entry recording credit purchase invoices

Purchase ledger: a ledger containing individual personal accounts for each credit supplier and recording all transactions with that supplier

Purchase order: a document used to place an order with a supplier

Purchase returns day book: book of original entry recording purchase credit notes

R

Rate of stock turnover: cost of sales dividend by average stock

Real accounts: a type of impersonal account relating to fixed assets

Realisable value: sale value

Realisation: revenue should not be recorded in the accounts until it is realised, i.e. when there is cash or the promise of cash

Reducing balance method: where the annual depreciation charge is based on the net book value of the fixed asset at the beginning of each financial period

Remittance advice: a document sent with a payment, advising the recipient which invoices etc., are being paid

Retained earnings for the year: the amount of net profit for the year that has not been distributed by the directors; it is the balance of the profit and loss appropriation account

Retained earnings: undistributed profits arising from the normal course of business

Return on capital employed: net profit in relation to capital invested (sole trader) or capital employed (limited company), expressed as a percentage. This is an important measure of profitability

Returned cheque: a cheque that has been paid into the bank, but not honoured by the drawer's bank (usually because of lack of funds)

Revaluation reserve: arises from the increase in value of a fixed asset above its net book value at the date of the revaluation. The reserve is a capital reserve and may not be used to finance the payment of cash dividends

Revenue expenditure: money spent on running costs that benefits only the current financial period

Revenue reserves: profits that arise from everyday trading activities and that can be distributed as dividends

Rights issue: an issue of shares for cash where the existing shareholders are offered the right to buy the shares usually at a price below market price

S

Sales day book: book of original entry recording credit sales invoices

Sales ledger: a ledger containing individual personal accounts for each credit customer and recording all transactions with that customer

Sales returns day book: book of original entry recording sales credit notes

Share premium: the amount paid for a share above its face value

Shareholders: the owners of a limited liability company

Shareholders' funds: the total of issued capital and all reserves

Sole trader: a business owned by one individual. The individual bears sole responsibility for the business's actions

Stakeholders: individuals, groups or organisations that have an interest in a business or are affected by the business. For example, employees, customers, suppliers, owners, investors, etc.

Standing order: where a fixed payment is made at regular intervals by the bank on the instructions of the business

Statement of account: a document sent to a customer detailing all recent transactions and informing them of the total amount outstanding

Straight-line method: where the annual depreciation charge is based on the cost of the fixed asset

Suspense account: a temporary account used to post a difference in the trial balance (i.e. the total of the debit side does not equal the total of the credit side) until such time as the differences are identified

 T

Trade discount: offered to businesses in a similar line of business, as distinct from the general public, often as an incentive for buying in bulk quantities

Trading account: calculates the gross profit made on sales by comparing the sales with the cost of sales

True and fair view: the principle that accounting records should be factually accurate wherever possible, or otherwise present a reasonable estimate of, or judgment about, the financial position

Turnover: means total sales – to be precise sales less returns in

 U

Unlimited liability: the owner of a business is fully responsible for all the debts of the business

Unpresented cheques: cheques that have been drawn and entered in the cash book, but have not yet been presented to the bank for payment

Index